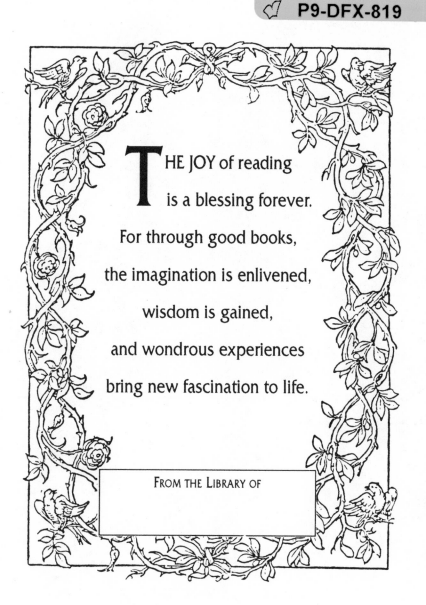

T HE JOY of reading
is a blessing forever.
For through good books,
the imagination is enlivened,
wisdom is gained,
and wondrous experiences
bring new fascination to life.

FROM THE LIBRARY OF

High-MAINTENANCE Relationships

LES PARROTT III PH.D.

Tyndale House Publishers, Inc.

WHEATON, ILLINOIS

AMERICAN ASSOCIATION OF
AACC
CHRISTIAN COUNSELORS

The American Association of Christian Counselors is an organization of professional, pastoral, and lay counselors committed to the promotion of excellence and unity in Christian counseling. The AACC provides conferences, software, video and audio resources, two professional journals, a resource review, as well as other publications and resources. Membership is open to anyone who writes for information: AACC, P.O. Box 739, Forest, VA 24551.

All Scripture quotations, unless otherwise indicated, are taken from the *Holy Bible,* New International Version®. Copyright© 1973, 1978, 1984 by International Bible Society. Used by permission of Zondervan Publishing House. All rights reserved. The "NIV" and "New International Version" trademarks are registered in the United States Patent and Trademark Office by International Bible Society. Use of either trademark requires permission of International Bible Society.

Scripture verses marked NEB are taken from *The New English Bible,* copyright© 1970, Oxford University Press, Cambridge University Press.

Scripture verses marked TLB are taken from *The Living Bible,* copyright© 1971 owned by assignment by KNT Charitable Trust. All rights reserved.

Designed by Raelee Edgar
Edited by Lynn Vanderzalm

Library of Congress Cataloging-in-Publication Data

Parrott, Les.
  High-maintenance relationships : how to handle impossible people / Les Parrott III.
    p. cm.
  ISBN 0-8423-1314-1 (alk. paper)
  1. Interpersonal relations.   I. Title.
HM132.P355   1996
302– dc20   96-7400

Printed in the United States of America

03 02 01 00 99 98 97 96
8   7   6   5   4   3   2

To the people who care so much about me—
despite the fact that I can be an impossible person
DOMINUS VOBISCUM

CONTENTS

ACKNOWLEDGMENTS

Thanks . . .

To my students and colleagues at Seattle Pacific University. You create a wonderful environment in which to work, learn, and live.

To Tim Clinton, who first brought me to Tyndale House Publishers and showed unflinching confidence in my ability to write.

To Gary Collins, who helped shape this book on a long flight between San Francisco and Hong Kong.

To Dawn Emleigh, Scott Titus, Doug Flather, Faye Smith, Nancy Scammacca, and all of the other AACC staff. You treat me with unparalleled kindness and personal care.

To Lori Nouguier and Tad Beckwith, who researched dozens of topics and retrieved hundreds of articles and books to help me on this project.

To my editor, Lynn Vanderzalm, who was amazingly gentle, genuinely supportive, and simply delightful throughout the writing process.

1

ARE YOU IN A HIGH-MAINTENANCE RELATIONSHIP?

IF YOU'RE like me, you never thought that maintaining relationships would be hard work. As a kid it never occurred to me to "work" on any of my relationships. They just happened. And if for any reason they didn't, I jumped ship. No fuss, no bother.

But somewhere along the line I entered the fray of mature relationships, and things got dicey. I learned that some people were more difficult, if not impossible, to get along with. I learned, for example, that trusted friends could betray me. Authority figures I admired could snub me. A colleague's constant criticism could hurt me. And even family members with important information could leave me out of the loop. But I also learned that, unless I wanted to be a hermit, I couldn't abandon every relationship that hit a snag.

The temptation to run from difficult relationships is still there. When impossible people get me down, I sometimes wish I were Daniel Defoe's Robinson Crusoe. Living alone on a desert island away from difficult people would be paradise. But Defoe's other writings snap me back to reality. "Though I don't like the crew," he wrote, "I won't sink the ship. In fact, in time of storm I'll do my best to save it. You see, we are all in this craft and must sink or swim together."

That's the rub with difficult people—we really do sink or swim together.

We encounter impossible people in our families, in our neighborhoods, in our churches, and in our workplace. When employees were asked "What upsets you most about where you work?" their number one complaint was about fellow workers. It turns out that job satisfaction depends more on our relationships than our salaries. Relationships make the difference between the job we love and the job we loathe.[1]

> Irritation in the heart of a believer is always an invitation to the devil to stand by.
> Eleanor Doan

But the importance of good relationships, of course, isn't limited to work settings. A pioneering band of researchers has studied the age-old mystery of what makes people happy, in a general sense, and their answer is not what you might expect. What comes up consistently at the top of the charts is not success, good looks, or any of those enviable assets. The clear winner is relationships. Close ones.[2]

Which brings me back to my point: If relationships make us so happy, why do so many of our relationships make life so difficult? And more importantly, what can we do to keep our cool, stand our ground, and reach positive solutions when we find ourselves in high-maintenance relationships, face-to-face with "impossible" people?

This book is my answer to that question.

PEOPLE WHO BEEF, BITE, AND BELLYACHE

About forty years ago, the U.S. Navy asked William Schutz to construct an instrument that would help them assemble compatible submarine crews, groups of men who could live together, elbow to elbow, for extended periods of time with minimum conflict among themselves. Schutz determined, not surprisingly, that compatible behavior was determined primarily by "natural fit." In other words, people who get along well with each other do so without much effort. Their relationship doesn't require much work; in fact, you could say it is low maintenance.

I hope that you have a few low-maintenance relationships, people with whom you naturally fit. Sure, you may hit temporary turbulence together from time to time, but it's periodic, and the relationship stays on course. If you are like most people, however, you also have some relationships that aren't so easy. These are the impossible people who beef, bite, and bellyache. They give you the cold shoulder, spread rumors, seethe with jealousy, play the victim, or trample your feelings. In

> **If it is possible, as far as it depends on you, live at peace with everyone.**
> Romans 12:18

some cases, they may be people you simply can't stand. To sum it up, these relationships require a lot of effort. They are your high-maintenance relationships.

When my wife, Leslie, and I first moved to Seattle some years ago, we lived in a city apartment with underground parking. One of our neighbors was a jet-setting businessperson who had a parking space next to ours. For the longest time, however, I didn't know what he drove— it was under wraps. Every time John parked his car, he sheathed it in a custom cover to protect the car's finish. One morning, however, as I pulled in to my space, I discovered what John was hiding. He was standing beside his automobile, with the hood up.

"Wow!" I said, ignoring his apparent plight as I rolled down my window and pulled into my space. "No wonder you take such good care of that thing," I exclaimed. It was a silver Jaguar XJ — something that was as shiny as a brand-new quarter.

"Yeah, well, I'm getting rid of it," John said with disgust.

"Why?"

"It's too finicky, and it takes all my time just keeping it up and running."

The same is true of high-maintenance relationships. Like an automobile that needs constant attention, they drain our energy, eat up our time, and create a stream of unnecessary hassles. Impossible people make life harder than it has to be. And high-maintenance relationships, like John's Jag, sometimes seem like more trouble than they're worth.

But before you think this is a book about writing off impossible people, think again. After combing libraries, listening to clients, surveying dozens of people, and practicing proven principles in my own life, I have concluded that it is possible to make most high-maintenance relationships work much better. In many cases you can make your high-maintenance relationships better than you could even imagine. As Scripture says, "If it is possible, as far as it depends on you, live at peace with everyone" (Rom. 12:18). The effort you exert to improve a difficult relationship is almost always rewarded with new vitality and personal strength. Other dividends include fewer worries, a clearer mind, a more positive outlook, a stronger sense of effectiveness, and better physical health. The bottom line is that improving your relationships makes your life easier.

> We are, each of us, angels with only one wing. And we can only fly embracing each other.
> Luciano de Cresenzo

If your life is free from clingy friends, aggressive employees, hypocritical colleagues, controlling relatives, indecisive coworkers, insensitive bosses, or any other descriptions that fall under "difficult people," read no further. Consider yourself blessed, and extremely rare. But if you deal with difficult people regularly, read on.

Let's start by examining your own situation for a moment. Just how much are the tensions in your relationships affecting you? What side effects are created by your high-maintenance relationships? Here's a test you can take to find out if any of your relationships are affecting your own personal and emotional health.

THE HIGH-MAINTENANCE SELF-TEST

By answering these questions you can assess whether or not you are in a high-maintenance relationship. Answer each item carefully and honestly.

Y   N   Do you feel especially anxious when a particular person has called and left a message for you to return the call?

Y N   Have you recently been dealing with a relationship that drains you of enthusiasm and energy?

Y N   Do you sometimes dread having to see or talk to a particular person at work or in a social situation?

Y N   Do you have a relationship in which you give more than you get in return?

Y N   Do you find yourself second-guessing your own performance as a result of an interaction with this person?

Y N   Do you become more self-critical in the presence of this person?

Y N   Is your creativity blocked, or is your clarity of mind hampered somewhat, by the lingering discomfort of having to deal with a difficult person?

Y N   Do you try to calm yourself after being with this person by eating more, biting your nails, or engaging in some other unhealthy habit?

Y N   Do you ever have imaginary conversations with this person or mental arguments in which you defend yourself or try to explain your side of a conflict?

Y N   Have you become more susceptible to colds, stomach problems, or muscle tension since having to deal with this difficult person?

Y N   Do you feel resentful that this person seems to treat other people better than she or he treats you?

Y N   Do you find yourself wondering why this person singles you out for criticism but rarely acknowledges things you do well?

Y N   Have you thought about quitting your job as a result of having to interact with this difficult person?

Y N   Have you noticed that you are more irritable or impatient with people you care about because of leftover frustrations from your interaction with this difficult person?

Y N   Are you feeling discouraged that this person has continued to drain you of energy despite your efforts to improve the relationship?

Scoring: Total the number of Ys you circled. If you circled ten or more Ys, you are certainly in a high-maintenance relationship.

IDENTIFYING YOUR IMPOSSIBLE PEOPLE

Everybody is somebody's impossible person some of the time. But rarely is somebody everyone's impossible person all of the time.

Think about that. Oh, we all can think of one or two people who seem to complicate everyone's existence, but those people are rare.

That's why a good rule of thumb is to remember that *the difficulty you experience with most impossible people is in your relationship, not in the person*. After all, someone you like very much might get along just fine with someone you cannot bear to be with. My wife and I have a mutual friend who, in my opinion, is blindly insensitive to others. Not according to Leslie, however. She gets along just fine with him. Impossibility, like beauty, is in the eye of the beholder.

When I decided to write this book, I immediately knew what kinds of people pushed my buttons and "deserved" to have chapters written about them (mostly because they reminded me of ugly traits I possessed!). Knowing, however, that I did not have a corner on impossible people, I surveyed more than one hundred people on the kinds of relationships they felt are the most difficult. I presented them with a list of two dozen high-maintenance relationships and asked them to rank their top five.

Give, and it will be given to you. A good measure, pressed down, shaken together and running over, will be poured into your lap. For with the measure you use, it will be measured to you.
Luke 6:38

Here is what I found: The most common complaints about difficult relationships center on people who are *critical and complaining* ("The Critic"). Next in line are people who are filled with *self-pity and play the victim* ("The Martyr"). Coming in at number three are people who are *automatically negative and pessimistic* ("The Wet Blanket"). In the number four slot are people who are *blindly insensitive to others* ("The Steamroller"). And rounding out the top five most common complaints about difficult people are those who *spread rumors and leak secrets* ("The Gossip").

Of the two dozen high-maintenance relationships on my list, however, more than these five stood out.[3] People repeatedly noted fifteen different types of high-maintenance relationships. And while the labels I give these fifteen relationships serve as shorthand here, they are not to be mistaken for caricatures. Each is a real-life relationship, portrayed as a human being, not a cartoon.

With this in mind, which of the following types sound like someone you know? From the following brief descriptions, rank your top five high-maintenance relationships (begin by placing a 1 next to the person who gives you the most grief—the person you would most like to know how to handle).

___**The Critic**— constantly complains and gives unwanted advice

___**The Martyr**— forever the victim and wracked with self-pity

___**The Wet Blanket**—pessimistic and automatically negative

___**The Steamroller**— blindly insensitive to others

___**The Gossip**—spreads rumors and leaks secrets

___**The Control Freak**— unable to let go and let be

___**The Backstabber**— irrepressibly two-faced

___**The Cold Shoulder**— disengages and avoids contact

___**The Green-Eyed Monster**— seethes with envy

___**The Volcano**— builds steam and is ready to erupt

___**The Sponge**— constantly in need but gives nothing back

___**The Competitor**— keeps track of tit for tat

___**The Workhorse**— always pushes and is never satisfied

___**The Flirt**— imparts innuendoes, which may border on harassment

___**The Chameleon**— eager to please and avoids conflict

Each of these fifteen high-maintenance relationships is the focus of a chapter in this book. You will probably want to read first about the ones you have marked before exploring others. Feel free. Each of these fifteen chapters is designed to be read independently, as a stand-alone resource that pinpoints strategies for a specific difficult person.

Before moving to these chapters, however, I want to make one point clear. *This is not a book about changing others as much as it is a book about changing yourself.* It is a book about learning skills for building better relationships. I often tell students in my college classes that relationships are a school for character, allowing the chance to study, in great detail and over time, temperaments very different from our own. The learning curve of relationships involves, to no small extent, filling out a picture of the other's limitations and making peace with the results.

If this is not a book about how to change difficult people, you might be wondering, then what is it? It is a book about growing as people and maintaining healthy relationships, even with people who seem to be impossible.

READING THIS BOOK FOR ALL IT'S WORTH

You don't have to let difficult personalities take control of your life. And you don't have to feel that your only option is a hasty exit. This book will show you a different way. Each of the fifteen chapters about specific high-maintenance relationships has a similar format. After some introductory remarks in each chapter, I outline the defining traits of the particular high-maintenance person. This is followed by a brief quiz that will help you identify whether you are in a relationship with this kind of person.

> We who are strong ought to bear with the failings of the weak and not to please ourselves.
> Romans 15:1

Next, I explain the dynamics underlying this person's behavior. We all want to know why someone behaves in an irritating way. What triggers the annoying behavior of the Backstabber, the Chameleon, the Gossip, or the Volcano? I take a look at how a person's background, demeanor, and motivations can explain his or her behavior.

The chapter then turns to practical ways of coping with the person. This subsection, by the way, almost always begins with a challenge to find some of the high-maintenance characteristics in yourself. I start with this point because you will be more patient with others once you see some of their traits in you. You will also have more empathy and, in turn, more grace to "do to others what you would have them do to you."

Each chapter then closes with a cross-reference to other high-maintenance relationships discussed in the book. Since no person is a pure prototype of any specific profile, this can serve as a simple suggestion to check out other possible helpful avenues of coping with this high-maintenance person.

2

THE CRITIC

*Constantly Complains and
Gives Unwanted Advice*

LAST Monday I dropped into my pastor's office unannounced. Tharon was leaning back in his chair with his feet propped up on his desk and with some papers in his hands.

"Did I catch you at a bad time?" I asked, sticking my head inside the doorway.

"Not at all," he replied. "Come in. Every Sunday I get a handful of anonymous Friendship & Worship cards from people who want to give me advice, and I'm just looking them over."

"I bet that's a blessing," I said sarcastically. We laughed as he read from anonymous cards complaining about everything from the lighting and temperature in the sanctuary to the music tempo and sermon topic. It seems some people, no matter what the setting, are bound to be critical.

As the survey I mentioned in the last chapter indicated, most people find that their number one high-maintenance relationships are with Critics. You know the type. They are the self-appointed nuisances who size you up and say you are too conservative, too liberal, too easygoing, too serious. They are the nit-picking boss, coworker, business partner, acquaintance, friend, and family member who second-guess your decisions and take pride in pointing out your mistakes. The tone of their voice conveys their disappointment in your misguided aspirations. And without raising a finger, they can shoot down every one of your good ideas. They have a wonderful plan for your life and can tell you every detail. Just ask. On second thought, just listen. They will tell you. They are Critics.

The boy will come to nothing.
Jakob Freud, about his son, Sigmund

I have always enjoyed reading biographies and learning about the struggles successful people overcome to achieve their goals. Invariably, successful people encounter Critics, usually by the score.

The manager of the Cleveland Indians, Tris Speaker, said of Babe Ruth: "He made a great mistake when he gave up pitching. Working once a week, he might have lasted a long time and become a great star." Jim Denny, manager of the Grand Ole Opry, fired Elvis Presley after a 1954 performance and said, "You ain't goin' nowhere . . . son. You ought to go back to drivin' a truck." The president of Decca Records said of the Beatles in 1962, "We don't like their sound. Groups of guitars are on the way out." Alan Livington, president of Capital Records, on the verge of the Beatles' first U.S. tour in 1964, said, "We don't think they'll do anything in this market."

Do you think Walt Disney faced any Critics? He was bankrupt when he went around Hollywood with his little "Steamboat Willie" cartoon idea. Can you imagine Disney trying to sell a talking mouse with a falsetto voice in the days of silent movies? Disney's dreams were large, and in spite of his critics, children around the world are grateful. People closest to him, in fact, believe Disney thrived on criticism. He was said to have asked ten people what they thought of a new idea, and if they were unanimous in their rejection of it, he would begin work on it immediately.

Whatever your feelings toward being criticized, don't expect to miss out. No matter how hard you work, how great your ideas, or how wonderful your talent, you probably will be the object of criticism. No one is exempt. Even the perfect motives of Jesus were often misunderstood, resulting in malicious criticism. I once read through the four Gospels and made a list of all the criticisms made against our Savior. They called Jesus a glutton (Matt. 11:19; Luke 7:34). They called him a drunkard (Matt. 11:19; Luke 7:34). They criticized Jesus for his association with sinners (Matt. 9:11; Mark 2:16; Luke 5:30). And worst of all, they called him a Samaritan, which was a sharp racial slur (John 8:48). Saying this was like accusing him of selling out to the enemy.

> **I care very little if I am judged by you or by any human court; indeed, I do not even judge myself.**
> 1 Corinthians 4:3

Maybe you face your Critics at work, maybe at church, maybe at home, but be assured, these high-maintenance people are everywhere. The good news is that unless you are a movie star, you don't have to read the reviews by your Critics in the *Chicago Tribune*. All you have to do is practice a few proven principles to manage this chronically critical person.

THE ANATOMY OF A CRITIC

Critics often find a cloud in the silver lining. You may think things are moving along quite nicely, but Critics are bound to find an error. This built-in negative detector is the hallmark of Critics. But several other traits characterize Critics: perfectionistic, driven, bossy, judgmental, power hungry, arrogant, exhausting, pedantic, and nitpicky.

Perfectionistic
"I'm married to the perfect man," said Claire. "The problem is, my husband expects me to be perfect too. And I'm not. After twenty-three years of marriage I'm not sure I can take any more of his criticism and rejection." Sadly, Critics' perfectionistic tendencies

bleed into nearly every relationship they have, and their high standards are the sure road to ruin. The smallest of infractions — a spot on a shirt, the dining table set incorrectly, the way furniture is arranged — can set off a tirade.

Driven

Surprisingly, Critics are usually pretty hard on themselves. They critique their own performance as much as anyone else's, and in turn their drivenness exceeds its limits. They want things done their way and will step into many situations to make sure things are done right. Push, push, push. Critics never seem to shut down.

Bossy

"My mother thinks she knows how to raise my kids better than I do," said a frustrated mother of three. "She doesn't just express her view. She insists that I follow her advice. Period." Many Critics, like this woman's mother, make their disapproval *very* clear and become not only overly critical but also interfering and bossy.

Judgmental

"My husband can't seem to hold back from criticizing me," a woman told me. "If it's not the meals I make — he thinks I should serve two vegetables at every meal — it's the fact that our kids go to bed later than he thinks they should. He makes me feel as if I'm a bad parent." Critics have a way of doing that. They sit on their self-designed throne, pass laws, and pronounce verdicts.

Power Hungry

There's something about the way Critics say, "I'm right, and you better believe I'm right" that makes even the most self-confident people start to question their own value. No doubt about it, Critics gain power through criticism. In his book *Control Theory*, psychologist William Glasser writes, "Nothing that we encounter leads to a greater and quicker loss of control than to be criticized. And, equally, it is harder to regain control when we are criticized than in any other situation."[1] Critics understand this and use every opportunity to arouse doubts in others by assuming a position of superiority.

Arrogant

Many critics are overly impressed with their own importance. They always assume the position of the expert. "I hope you are not thinking of putting that there," they will snap. "Surely you didn't think I would overlook this." Critics seldom ask questions. Instead, they assume the posture of the all-knowing expert on almost every subject.

Exhausting

"My boss is a nitpicker. When something goes wrong, it always has to be someone's fault—and that usually means mine. He calls it 'constructive criticism' and claims I'm overly sensitive. But his criticism wears me down. I come home each afternoon exhausted from his complaints." If you can identify with this statement, you know what it's like to deal with Critics. They are exhausting.

Pedantic

Critics are born teachers. They parade their knowledge in front of others and focus on trivial details of learning. "Wait just a minute," they might interrupt, "don't you remember what we learned about driving downtown at this hour?" Critics have a way of making you feel as if you are back in grade school, and they are holding the grade book.

Nitpicky

People who sell cars know what "wheel kickers" are. They are the people who never buy a car because they are so picky about every little detail. Wheel kickers listen to the motor and hear a knock nobody else hears. They see minor upholstery imperfections that nobody else would notice. Critics are often just as picky as wheel kickers.

DO YOU KNOW A CRITIC?

The following self-test can help you assess whether you are in a high-maintenance relationship with a Critic. Identify the person or people who have come to your mind as you have read the preceding paragraphs. Circle the *Y* if the statement is true of the person or people about whom you are thinking. Circle the *N* if the statement does not apply to this person or people.

Y N   This person is sometimes an arrogant know-it-all.

Y N   If there is a flaw to be found, this person will definitely find it.

Y N   Being around this person is often like being on trial.

Y N   This person has no problem telling people what, when, and how to do just about anything.

Y N   I sometimes feel as if I am with my third-grade teacher when I am with this person.

Y N   This person's endless complaining is exhausting.

Y N   I sometimes feel inferior around this person because of the constant critiques.

Y N   This person is bossy.

Y N   If I have something on my face or clothes, this person will not be the most tactful in helping me remove it.

Y N   This person is often in the teaching mode.

Y N   I can count on this person complaining or pointing out a flaw about something nearly every day.

Y N   This person seems to carry most of the power in our relationship.

Y N   In choosing five terms to describe this person, *critical* would be among them.

Y N   I often feel defensive around this person.

Y N   Even when I think things are going smoothly, this person will find a problem.

Scoring: Total the number of Ys you circled. If you circled ten or more Ys, you are certainly in a high-maintenance relationship with a Critic.

UNDERSTANDING CRITICS

They don't like the way you drive. Or park. They get nervous when you handle their CDs. You would think their own ranting would wear them down. But like the Energizer bunny, they just keep going and going and going. The question is *why?* Why are Critics addicted to criticism?

Critics often believe their criticism is helpful. They believe the myth that it is possible to help people by denouncing their faults—even

without being asked to do so. "I don't want to criticize but . . . ,"
you will hear Critics say. What Critics don't realize is that their
attempts at reformation often induce the opposite of what they
hope. When we hear criticism, our first instinct is to defend
ourselves against the criticism, not to change. Most true change
occurs not as the result of criticism but in quiet recollection or
with someone who patiently cares.

Critics are often motivated by a simple desire to solve problems. They
see something wrong and blurt out a solution that
ends up sounding more critical than helpful. "I
can't believe you don't have an extension cord on
this thing." "Some weed killer would take care of
the problem in your yard." "I hope you exercise if
you eat that kind of food." Critics don't screen
their thoughts or soften their critiques. Their advice—wanted or not—just rolls off their tongue in an attempt to
solve problems.

> **The strength of criticism lies in the weakness of the thing criticized.**
> Henry Wadsworth Longfellow

Critics often feel it is their duty to find something wrong. They
cannot rest or relax until some probing uncovers something for
which they can find fault. Even if you do an excellent job, many
Critics will still need to find something to complain about. It's part
of Critics' nature.

Some Critics see their criticism as merely "letting it all hang out."
This is especially destructive in marriage relationships. Some
spouses show respect to everyone *except* their own spouse. I've
worked with clients who treat colleagues with kid gloves and then
go home and mercilessly pick on their spouse. One woman exhausted herself pleasing people and being polite at work; but once
she was home, she spoke to her husband any way she wanted,
using vulgarities freely or barking orders at him.

Many Critics were raised to be critical. Marcie, for example, was
raised by a mother who was struggling to make ends meet as a
single parent. Abandoned by her husband, this single mother
faced the world with a chip on her shoulder. Her resentment
spread to everything she did. Since Marcie was Lucy's only child,
Marcie got an earful of her mother's complaints. As a child, Marcie
was powerless to change her situation and was forced to listen to

her mother's endless harangues. Lucy would maintain a perpetual commentary on everyone, male or female, acquaintance or stranger. Marcie grew up believing that this behavior was normal. She contracted her "nagaholism" from her mother, and without any awareness that a running monologue riddled with judgment and criticisms was not desirable, she perpetuated the tradition.

Whatever the dynamics underlying Critics' character, it is important to understand that Critics fall along a continuum. In other words, all Critics are not the same. At one end of the continuum is the mean-spirited Critic who suffers from such a fragile self-esteem that he or she compulsively cuts down everyone. This Critic is like a toxin in a home or organization. At the other end of the continuum is the person who feels genuinely responsible for your welfare. These are Critics who might butt in where they aren't welcome, but they are sincere and deserve our attention. With this understanding, you will be better equipped to handle this often difficult and trying high-maintenance relationship.

When the radio was invented, experts said it had no future.

COPING WITH CRITICS

It's difficult to stay objective about Critics. Sometimes we feel they're needles in a balloon factory. But at the same time, some Critics can also offer helpful suggestions. The trick is learning to separate the good from the bad. The following principles can help you manage your high-maintenance relationships with Critics and learn a little more about yourself in the process.

Face the Critic Within

A team of sociologists interviewed every resident in a mill town in New England. Among other things, they learned that each person admitted criticizing other men and women in the community. But each person was scandalized to learn he or she was in turn criticized by others. This double standard is universal. We pass quick opinions on what other people do or say, but we are aghast to learn we are the butt of somebody else's criticism. So let's face it. We are all a little critical. Who hasn't nagged someone for something at some time? What spouse has never used criticism as a means of persuasion? What parent has never criticized a child's embarrassing behavior? We are all part Critic, and we will begin to make progress with Critics only when we come to terms with the Critic within.

Put Yourself in the Critics' Shoes

Facing the Critic within will certainly help you empathize with your Critics, but you can go a step further by trying to walk in the shoes of your Critics. I lived for several years in the shadow of a beloved professor whom I revered. I valued his opinions, and I wanted him to be proud of my work. When the two of us were together, however, he was far more likely to punish than praise. I would invariably leave our conversations depleted and wondering why I couldn't seem to please him. Then I ran into Ned, a former student of this same man. Ned helped me realize that our professor had come from a terrible home situation that no child should have to endure, a situation in which he was never, ever affirmed by his parents. As I learned more about my professor's background, I was able to let his criticism roll off my back more easily. Of course I would still love to hear him affirm my writing or some other aspect of my ministry, but it is far less important to me today because I understand a little more about the person.

> It is only as we fully understand opinions and attitudes different from our own and the reasons for them that we better understand our own place in the scheme of things.
> S. I. Hayakawa

Don't Close Your Ears

The greatest temptation in relating to Critics is tuning them out. Most children, for example, have mastered this strategy. We psychologists call it "mommy deafness," a sudden, temporary inability to hear any request a mother makes. Indeed, children can notice the tinkle of an ice-cream truck a block away, but they can't hear their mom right in front of them. You and I do the same thing. But we are missing something when we completely tune out what our Critics say. Why? Because sometimes they are right! Our Critics may know something we don't know. In referring to Critics in his life, E. Stanley Jones said, "They are the unpaid watchmen of my soul."[2] The best way to keep your ears open is to paraphrase the complaints your Critics make in order to confirm that you understand what they are saying to you. Say, "Let me be sure I've understood you. You are saying . . ." Repeat the complaint in your own words, then ask the Critics for confirmation. Be open to hearing what your Critics have to say. However, when you perceive that complaints come from blatantly mean-spirited Critics, who question authority by reflex and howl out of habit, tune them out. Their criticisms say more about them than about you.

Limit the Criticism You'll Accept

Have you ever let one critical person keep you from recognizing the strength of the hundred who are in agreement with you? I have. As a professor, for example, I know that when a student is critical of my teaching, I can end up focusing all of my emotional energy on that single student. Nothing could be worse for me and the other students in the classroom. I have always admired the way Billy Graham has handled his Critics. They may say whatever they will, but he does not let their criticism deter him from his goal of preaching the gospel. I know a business executive who puts up with his share of criticism, and he finally came to the conclusion that he would accept criticism only from people who had something to gain from his success. That's a bit limiting for me, but we can all benefit from the principle. The apostle Paul certainly did. He wrote to Timothy about one of his Critics, Alexander the metalworker, who did him "a great deal of harm." Eventually, Paul concluded, "I was delivered from the lion's mouth. The Lord will rescue me from every evil attack and will bring me safely to his heavenly kingdom" (2 Tim. 4:14, 17-18). If you have a Critic picking away at the minutiae and keeping you from your primary task, set your boundaries. Consult a friend who can help you sort the minor criticisms from the major ones.

Here is a glutton and a drunkard, a friend of tax collectors and "sinners."
Matthew 11:19

Tame Your Inner Gremlin

We all have "soft spots," areas that are particularly vulnerable and sensitive. When Critics approach these areas, we go into red alert. Critics activate our critical voice within. In his book *Taming Your Gremlin*, family therapist Richard Carson seeks to identify that inner narrator who puts us down and tries to convince us that whatever Critics say is true. Carson calls that voice our "gremlin." So to keep your gremlin from raising its head, guard your soft spots carefully around Critics. Declare your soft spots off-limits. Say, "You may evaluate or critique anything I do, but don't tell me how to correct the relationship with my sister. For right now, that is my business, not yours."

Institute a "Complaint Session"

If the chronic complaining from the Critics in your life upsets you and interferes with your ability to work or simply relax at home, try setting aside a specific time for them to vent complaints. When Critics start to whine, say something like, "I can tell you're upset. Can we talk about your concerns at lunch [or in ten minutes or after the meeting]?" Then follow through by giving Critics time to vent their frustrations. Help them to limit their whining to that time period, and agree on it in advance. Surprisingly, Critics are

Blame is safer than praise.
Ralph Waldo Emerson

usually open to such a strategy. It taps into their problem-solving mentality and provides a guaranteed forum in which to be heard. It also protects you from feeling that you could be bombarded by complaining and critiquing at any moment. So if it feels right, institute a complaint session with your Critics.

Put Things in Perspective

One of the hard parts of living or working with Critics is that we often care about what they say about us. To gloss over their comments is to be in denial. We want people to think good things of us. But we can decrease the impact of the negative commentary if we put it into perspective. The apostle Paul declared his own free- dom from Critics this way: "I care very little if I am judged by you or by any human court" (1 Cor. 4:3). He was telling some meddlesome Corinthian Chris- tians to get off his back, and we can learn from his

Everyone told Renoir to give up painting because he had no talent.

example. Freely translated, it comes to this: "What you say and what you think about me matters to me. But after I have wrestled with my own conscience, after I have consulted my own convictions, and after I have made my decisions, your judgment will not matter much. It matters some, but not much. I will not let the appraisal of critical people tell me how to feel about what I am and what I do. I will not rest my case with Critics."

Keep Your Dreams Alive

Perhaps the deadliest poison of criticism comes when it is aimed toward someone's aspirations. Years ago, the sister of an innovative college professor suffered from a hearing deficiency. In the midst of building a device to help her hear better, he invented an unusual contraption. After many years of trial and error and eventual success, the professor was ready to take the device into production. He traveled extensively to gain financial backing for his dream. But everywhere he went, potential supporters laughed at his idea that the human voice could be carried along a wire. The professor could have allowed his Critics to discourage him. He could have given up, but he didn't. And nobody laughs at Alexander Graham Bell today.

> **You, then, why do you judge your brother? Or why do you look down on your brother? For we will all stand before God's judgment seat.**
> Romans 14:10

Don't allow your Critics to snuff out your dreams. Protect yourself from this folly by associating with people who support and nurture your ideas. Keep your dreams alive.

Understand the Critical Gender Difference

It seems that women get labeled "nags" far more often than men do. But according to Deborah Tannen, author of the best-selling book *You Just Don't Understand: Women and Men in Conversation*, that may be due to the different ways men and women have been raised.[3] Women are brought up to please others and to equate fulfilling requests with showing love. Men, on the other hand, equate receiving requests with taking orders, and they react accordingly: "Stop telling me what to do!" Consequently, when a woman's husband fails to do what she has asked, she feels hurt or puzzled. So she asks again. And again. But each time she reminds him of her request, he feels more resistant. He often waits before doing what his wife has requested so that he feels that he is responding out of his own free will—and not because he's been told to. So if you are married to a Critic, remember this fundamental gender difference.

Beware of the Critic's Triangle

Some Critics express their complaining in fairly destructive ways. Instead of criticizing you to your face, they complain about you to other people, creating a triangle of three people who become involved in the critical process. Much like Gossips, these Critics review your performance in front of your colleagues when you are not present. You can usually detect these Critics by the remarks they make about others when they are with you. You may let down your guard because these people make you feel as if you are one of their dearest confidants. The truth is that you, along with almost everyone else, are a target of their criticism. When you are with these kinds of Critics, stay low and move fast.

To avoid criticism do nothing, say nothing, be nothing.
Elbert Hubbard

Know Your Toughest Critic . . . and Accept His Grace

Our ultimate and toughest critic is someone who knows us only too well: God. He knows everything. The psalmist says: "You have examined my heart and know everything about me. . . . You know my every thought. . . . You know what I am going to say before I even say it" (Ps. 139:1-2, 4, TLB). God has our phone tapped. He knows our motives, our plans, our excuses. Nietzsche wrote a story about a man who in desperation killed God. When people asked the man why he had killed God, the man replied, "He knew too much." We cannot escape God's watchful eye. Yet because of God's grace we do not have to live in fear of him. We can get to know him and be made free. This was Paul's secret; he knew his Divine Critic in a way that made him free, for he met God at the cross and saw that our God judged his own Son in our place. On the cross God's accusing finger, once pointed at us, was changed into an open hand outstretched to us. Our Judge became our Savior. Our ultimate Critic became our Best Friend.

The rule in carving holds good as to criticism; never cut with a knife what you can cut with a spoon.
Charles Buxton

CROSS-REFERENCE

For more information related to Critics, see these other high-maintenance relationships: the Backstabber, the Control Freak, the Gossip, and the Wet Blanket.

3
THE MARTYR
Forever the Victim and
Wracked with Self-Pity

DEALING with Martyrs was cited in the survey as the second-most-difficult relationship. We all have days when we feel a bit like a martyr, days when self-pity descends on us. For most people, self-pity is fleeting, a reminder that life isn't always fair.

But for some people self-pity can be like an infection: If it's not caught early and treated aggressively, it can become chronic, leading people to feel continually like victims.

Such is the case for Martyrs. They can be knocked over by the tiniest difficulties—a burned dinner, a lonely weekend, a traffic jam—and show little interest in getting up. Like a flower flattened by a strong wind, Martyrs stay down. Hopelessly and helplessly they give in to real and imagined unfairness and refuse the helping hand of a friend: "Oh, don't worry about me. I'm fine," or "You don't have time for my troubles. You just go ahead." Martyrs feel spurned by the world. They often refuse help and are burned at their own stake.

It doesn't take much to become a Joan or John of Arc. Mothers can overburden themselves with household chores, then say, "No one really cares about me. As far as my family is concerned, I'm just a slave."

Fathers can use the same approach: "I work my fingers to the bone, and no one cares. Everyone uses me."

Vicky is a typical Martyr. With her soft-spoken manner you barely notice she is in the room. She suffers from excruciating back pain, and at times she can barely sit up for more than five minutes at a stretch. But she refuses a friend's offer to clean her apartment and cook dinner. "I've got to manage alone," she says, "because I can't expect someone else to be here every minute of every day."

> **I think the most uncomfortable thing about martyrs is that they look down on people who aren't.**
> Samuel N. Behrman

Vicky refuses help but feels all the more persecuted when her friends don't stop by. Like every other Martyr, Vicky wallows in self-pity. It has become so insidious to her soul that she is all but entrapped. Her friends fear she will never emerge to live a fun, contented life. And her woeful existence is becoming increasingly exhausting for even her family members and most dedicated companions.

If you have Martyrs in your life, you have seen firsthand how their wallowing can go on and on. Solutions to their problems, no matter how powerful, can't seem to penetrate their complaining. Martyrs are locked tight in a victim chamber. But that doesn't mean you need to suffer too. You can use several effective strategies for living and working with confirmed Martyrs, even when they refuse to be rescued.

THE ANATOMY OF A MARTYR

Unfortunately, Martyrs are all too prevalent in our society. Turn on any morning or afternoon talk show, and you will see people who are stuck in a bad marriage or who are too fat or too miserable to deal with life. You will also hear them blame their parents, their schooling, their income, their siblings, their friends, their church, their government, and, of course, themselves. What dynamics do Martyrs have in common? They are defeated, passive, self-blaming, helpless, irrational, broody, and worrisome.

Defeated

Everyone whines a little in response to life's small irritations: you have an acne outbreak at the worst time; you lose your keys; you get stood up for an appointment. Who wouldn't feel a little defeated? But most of us are able to stop feeling negative, recover our equilibrium, and get on with living. Not so for Martyrs. They give up quickly and suffer long-lasting defeat. The Old Testament prophet Jonah expressed his discouragement and sense of defeat. Even after the inhabitants of Nineveh repented, Jonah said, "Now, O Lord, take away my life, for it is better for me to die than to live" (Jon. 4:3).

Passive

If one were to coin a battle cry for Martyrs, it would be "I can't!" I can't lose weight. I can't get a promotion. I can't change. I can't meet new friends. Martyrs make little effort to rally against down-beat thoughts. And rarely do they ask for or accept help, even—or especially—when that help is freely and lovingly offered. Martyrs may desperately need help, but they will still rebuff a gesture of caring.

Self-Blaming

In his book *When Bad Things Happen to Good People,* Rabbi Harold Kushner tells of paying condolence calls on the families of two women who died of natural causes. At the first home, the son of the deceased woman told the rabbi: "If only I had sent my mother to Florida and gotten her out of this cold, she would be alive today. It's my fault she died." At the second home, the son told the rabbi: "If only I hadn't insisted on my mother's going to Florida, she would be alive today. It's my fault that she's dead." Martyrs, like these sons, are often addicted to self-blame.

Helpless

There is an old joke about a farmer. As he stands in his field, he sees a man on a horse galloping swiftly along the road. The farmer calls out, "Hey, where are you going?" The rider turns around and shouts back, "Don't ask me; ask my horse." Martyrs, like this rider, feel as if they are no longer masters over their own destiny. They have given up the reins and appear to be utterly helpless.

Irrational

Martyrs often feel as if they are doomed. Many times, however, they are relatively fortunate. In the based-on-fact movie *Reversal of Fortune*, both von Bulows are first-class Martyrs. Claus feels sorry for himself because he's worth only a million dollars while his wife has eight million. She also beats herself up because her unfaithful husband wants a divorce. Totally blind to their real situation, the privileged blue bloods sink deeper and deeper into chemical dependence and genuine tragedy.

Broody

Martyrs often feel unchecked broodiness, which prompts a string of demoralizing thoughts and further gloom. When Julia goes to dinner with Maria and her father, Maria's dad wears a suit. Julia finds herself getting moody at dinner and says to Maria later, "When I look at your dad, I know why you are so successful. He is so handsome. And he wears a suit to dinner. You are so lucky. My dad stumbles around in polka-dot shorts. He's never been a good parent. It makes me wonder if I'll ever have a chance in life. With a dad like him, how can I expect to succeed at anything?"

Worrisome

Devotional writer A. W. Tozer said something every Martyr could take to heart: "If only we would stop lamenting and look up. God is here. Christ is risen. All this we know as theological truth. It remains for us to turn it into a joyous spiritual experience." Martyrs are perpetual worriers who are distracted from the truth. They make up scenarios in advance, convinced that they will have a horrible time at a party, that nobody will talk to them, and that everything will go wrong before they even step out of the house. Martyrs, as the saying goes, put up their umbrellas long before it rains.

DO YOU KNOW A MARTYR?

The following self-test can help you assess whether you are in a high-maintenance relationship with a Martyr. Identify the person or people who have come to your mind as you have read the preceding paragraphs. Circle the *Y* if the statement is true of the person or people about whom you are thinking. Circle the *N* if the statement does not apply to this person or people.

Y N If life has a plan, this person feels as if he or she isn't in on it.

Y N This person feels defeated before even entering the competition.

Y N This person wallows in self-pity.

Y N Whatever advice is offered, this person has a reason why it won't work.

Y N It is as if this person has raised the white flag to surrender to life.

Y N People would characterize this person as worrisome.

Y N This person feels as if he or she has been cursed.

Y N This person is often not rational about problem solving.

Y N This person doesn't see his or her life situation in realistic terms.

Y N This person's general attitude is "Poor me."

Y N This person feels as if everyone else has it better than he or she does.

Y N This person is doing nearly nothing to find solutions for his or her problems.

Y N This person can often be heard saying, "If only . . ."

Y N This person is wracked with self-blame, which spills onto others.

Y N This person appears utterly helpless.

Scoring: Total the number of *Y*s you circled. If you circled ten or more *Y*s, you are certainly in a high-maintenance relationship with a Martyr.

UNDERSTANDING MARTYRS

I recently read an article about defeat and its physiological effects on the nervous system; the accompanying photo showed a rat thwarted in its effort to climb out of a bowl while other rats around the bowl were eating a variety of tasty foods. That is a good picture of how Martyrs feel— trapped at the bottom of a vast chasm while the rest of the world is having a party. Strangely, Martyrs almost always refuse help. By all appearances, they want to be left to their own devices, eventually giving up and crying "Poor me." This strange behavior seems completely absurd to most people, but Martyrs have their reasons.

Martyrs feel diminished by whatever they accept from others. Why? Because they often experience anxiety at the very times when most of us experience pleasure and a sense of security. Many Martyrs have trouble learning from others, even simple things like learning to cook. At the root of this resistance is a strong need for control and a fear of dependency. The greater the need, the harder Martyrs will fight anyone who tries to help.

When Sarah, age thirty-three, was laid off from her teaching job during a round of citywide budget cuts, her friend Roy watched helplessly while her car was repossessed. He offered several times to lend her money for the payments, but she refused. "She wouldn't even accept a loan with a written agreement to pay me back with interest," he recalls. "When I would ask her why, she would just say 'because'— like a child. I watched her waste hours taking the awful bus system to job interviews. We nearly broke up over this because I figured that her refusal meant that she didn't feel close enough to me to accept any help. But then I found out that she had also turned down a loan from her closest female friend. I finally realized that whatever was going on, it had nothing to do with me."

Roy was right. When Martyrs resist caring gestures, it usually means that they are anxious, not that they don't like the caring person. In Sarah's case, she decided long ago never to accept anything from anybody. She was raised by parents who used money as a way of controlling their children's lives. And when

> **A great many people seem to embalm their troubles. I always feel like running away when I see them coming.**
>
> Dwight L. Moody

Sarah was in college, her father stopped his financial support because she switched from a prelaw program to one in English education. "My policy from that time on," says Sarah, "was never to take anything from anyone, because there are always going to be strings attached."

Sarah is typical of most Martyrs. She was set up in childhood, and as an adult, she can't tell the difference between help that's offered out of a desire to dominate and help that's offered out of love. When she was a child, she could see no difference.

Sarah's story points out another underlying dynamic of Martyrs. *Martyrs are stuck in a mind-set that sees no middle ground between lone-wolf independence and childlike helplessness.* "I know this isn't rational," says Robert, "but even a little bit of help makes me feel like a baby. I broke my arm last year and refused to let my wife pump the gas into our car, even though she often did this before I broke my arm. I put it in terms of concern for her. I told her I didn't want her pumping gas because she had too much to do taking care of all the things I couldn't do. But the truth is that I hated the feeling of not being in control."

> **Let us hold unswervingly to the hope we profess, for he who promised is faithful.**
> Hebrews 10:23

Martyrs fear losing control. Robert is healthy enough to view his own behavior with a fair amount of detachment. But in most Martyrs, self-sufficiency masks serious problems, problems that are only exacerbated by the emotional isolation that Martyrs impose on themselves. "You find that 'I can handle it myself' mentality in people in all sorts of desperate trouble," says Carla Perez, author of *Getting Off the Merry-Go-Round.* [1] "Rather than admit they need help from other human beings, these people turn to destructive habits— drugs, alcohol, any kind of self-medication for emotional pain— to maintain the illusion of being in charge. Control is the overwhelming issue."

In some instances, Martyrs' need for control manifests itself not as self-sufficiency but as self-sacrifice. They do everything for everyone else and seem to want nothing in return. However, then they often whine about the unfairness of those who lean on them. These Martyrs enjoy collecting grievances. Always being the giver rather than the receiver puts them in a powerful position; they add up what they think other people owe them but act as if it doesn't really matter. But if it doesn't really matter, why do all of the people around them feel so guilty?

Fear of rejection is another feeling Martyrs battle. While a few Martyrs may look like Control Freaks, their unwillingness to ask for help or receive anything from others can be a cover for hurt, fear, or a deep sense of feeling unworthy. They learned in childhood that their needs weren't important, so they end up thinking that they don't deserve anything nice. Many times they will say this out loud when they're presented with something wonderful. They'll clearly say, "I don't deserve this."

Annie, a junior in college, assumed her boyfriend was insincere when he first used the I-don't-deserve-this line. "I had given him two tickets to a baseball game," she told me. "I thought his comment was his idea of something polite to say. Then, when I realized he was genuinely uncomfortable, I didn't know what to think." When Annie and her boyfriend became engaged, she met his family and understood why he had such trouble receiving anything. "His mother," she said, "has some really weird ideas about spoiling children." She went on to describe how on every birthday, his mother would send a check to one of the charities in her son's name after telling him he was "such a lucky little boy that he didn't need anything." Naturally he feels guilty when someone does something nice for him. As Annie said, "He was brought up to believe that it's morally wrong to accept a gift you don't absolutely need."

> **Surrendering to despair is man's favorite pastime. God offers a better plan, but it takes effort to grab it and faith to claim it.**
> Charles R. Swindoll

I have known people who played the Martyr role in a family or work setting, taking all the pain and all the blame and none of the help. Some were wives of alcoholics, drug addicts, or compulsive gamblers. Some were men or women whose spouses abused them physically or psychologically, beating them with fists or words. But many Martyrs I have met are the ordinary people who forever feel as if they are the victims of perceived injustice.

COPING WITH MARTYRS

Not a single microchip in the American Psychological Association's computer bank, research project on its roster, or self-help book on its resource list is devoted to the malady of martyrdom. But every therapist is familiar with this condition. Let's explore several ways you can handle the Martyrs in your life.

Face the Martyr Within

"The current idea of 'no negative feelings' is unnatural," writes Lesley Hazleton, author of *The Right to Feel Bad*. "We're made to feel we should be able to move with ease from job to job, one home to another, one age to the next, never taking time to feel the emptiness of loss."[2] I agree. When it comes to experiencing an emotion we despise in someone else, we are all the more likely to run from it in ourselves. However, we all feel self-pity sometimes, and we may even enjoy the lonely act of refusing another's kind-

> **He that despairs degrades God.**
> Owen Feltham

ness. Haven't you ever asked for some time alone, some time to be by yourself on your awful, no good, rotten day? Sure, we all have moments of saying "Poor me." Tap into this feeling to muster up a little empathy for the Martyrs in your life. It will help you ease the tension.

Don't Expect Much Change

Most Martyrs are stuck in a rut. They were raised with self-pity and weaned on guilt. So if you are going to remain involved with such people, lower your expectations. Martyrs change slowly. Most of the time, their transformation occurs gradually through much psychotherapy. This means that for your own well-being, you can't impose a standard that is unattainable. When it comes to presenting Martyrs with a gift, for example, you have to get your pleasure from the act of giving itself and not rely on the Martyr's reaction. The reaction probably won't be a burst of joy. Get the idea? Lower your expectations, and you will lower your level of frustration.

Get Martyrs Laughing

Let's face it, Martyrs aren't the life of the party. They can be downright downers. After all, they are unhappy about the pain in their life but at the same time seem resigned to it and reluctant to change it. In many cases Martyrs seem to believe they deserve to suffer. As with the Puritans, life for Martyrs is grim, serious business. The Puritans, in fact, actually passed laws against laughing on Sunday. Someone once defined a Puritan as a person who would abolish bullfighting not because it caused the bull pain but because it gave the spectators pleasure. Martyrs understand. But that doesn't mean you can't do your best to yuk it up with an uptight Martyr. Take every opportunity you have to add a little comic relief to the life of Martyrs. It will ease your relationship, and it is probably one of the most sacred gifts you could give. Scottish writer George Macdonald once said, "It is the heart that is not yet sure of its God that is afraid to laugh in his presence." Laughter not only will bring you and Martyrs a little closer to each other, it also will bring Martyrs a little closer to God.

Stay Clear of Advice

Trying to give advice to Martyrs is like trying to talk a police officer out of a ticket after you have run a red light. It's futile. Martyrs always answer with "Yes, but . . ." and proceed to tell

> It is the cause and not merely the death that makes the martyr.
> Napoleon Bonaparte

you why their problems won't submit to your solutions. Nothing you can do or say will change their predicament. "I have given my friend Ronda one successful example after the next about people who were unemployed but ended up finding good jobs," said Karen. "But she just won't hear it." The truth is that Ronda hears it but doesn't want to act on it. As a confirmed Martyr, Ronda would rather whine about her crummy job than find a new one. Perhaps she feels she doesn't deserve any better. Maybe she fears failing. Whatever the reason, she, like many other Martyrs, doesn't heed anyone's advice. So don't bang your head against the wall repeatedly trying to solve a Martyr's problems with good advice. After the first few suggestions (you have to at least try it), you are wasting your breath. In his best-selling book *The Road Less Traveled*, Dr. Scott Peck writes about the tendency of Martyrs to give their free will away by shunning advice. "Sooner or later, if they are to be healed, they must learn that the entirety of one's adult life is a series of personal choices, decisions. If they can accept this totally, then they become free people. To the extent they do not accept this, they will forever feel themselves victims."[3]

Find the Problem, If You Can

For some reason or another, Martyrs believe malevolent forces are picking on them. Like a spaniel whacked with a newspaper, they usually don't know why they are being "punished." They just know that they are getting a raw deal. If you are patient with friends who are Martyrs, however, you may be able to crack the code and solve the mystery. When your friends complain that nothing ever goes right, you can reply, "Tell me about that. What exactly hasn't gone right?" This kind of gentle probing can reveal the real or imagined thorn that is most irritating Martyrs. By becoming aware of it — in specific terms — they may end up doing something about it. You see, helpless people tend to generalize their negative feeling, which clouds everything. By helping them pinpoint their real problem, you are raising their awareness and bringing them closer to a place of action.

Avoid the Guilt Trap

Martyrs, in addition to blaming themselves, often blame the weather, their business, their childhood, and even you! Forever the victim, they enjoy self-pity and seek the pity of others with their poor-helpless-me routine. In other words, Martyrs are masters of inducing guilt. After all, it is easy to feel that you are somehow not doing enough to help them through their pain or that you could and should do more. The truth is that you can never do enough. So accept this fact, and avoid a painful guilt trip.

Know the Difference between Self-Pity and Depression

Martyrs' self-pity is not the same as depression, but the two are very similar: Sufferers of both lose interest in their former pleasures, are overrun by dark thoughts, and are plagued by a sense of futility. Both are likely to be found languishing at home alone, cradled by their old reliable couch. The big difference between depression and self-pity is that the former is much deeper and more dangerous. If the Martyrs in your life have lost interest or pleasure in almost all usual activities and pastimes and if their mood is affecting their appetite, sleep, or concentration, they may more likely be suffering from depression. Other symptoms may include tearfulness, irritability, and excessive feelings of worthlessness and hopelessness. If you suspect the Martyrs in your life are suffering from depression, urge them to seek professional help. By the way, generally speaking, depressed people are much more open to seeking help than are nondepressed Martyrs.

Keep Your Tank Full

"I used to spend hours listening to stories about Sue's terrible life," says Linda. "Her uncle was suing her for her grandfather's money, and her mother took the uncle's side. Sue was such a wreck over the whole thing that she blew her entire inheritance on a month-long shopping binge." But after a while, Linda began to feel exploited. "Sue never thanked me for listening, and she never asked me a thing about my life. Just thinking about being with Sue right now leaves me limp." Relating to Martyrs can drain you of energy. If you have ever endured an evening with one of these difficult people, you probably wound up feeling as if you had been submerged in Elmer's glue. Martyrs can't discuss anything other than their melancholia— which spills onto, sticks to, and exhausts anyone who'll listen. Because of this, you need to take special care to avoid being depleted of your own energy when you are around Martyrs. Note how much time you are spending with them, and monitor your energy level. Before long, you will have a good sense of how much you can endure before you need to break away and refuel.

CROSS-REFERENCE

For more information related to Martyrs, see these other high-maintenance relationships: the Chameleon, the Sponge, the Wet Blanket, and the Workhorse.

4

THE WET BLANKET

Pessimistic and Automatically
Negative

"EVERY time I walked through the door to my boss's office, I felt wobbly," says Vanessa, a twenty-nine-year-old magazine editor. "Her negativism filled the room like a poison."

In the beginning, Vanessa attended editorial meetings full of high spirits and ideas. But, faced with a cynical superior who set a deadly tone for these sessions, "it didn't take long before my mood plummeted. And I wasn't the only one. Other editors would slink out of the meetings with their chins on their chests."

Do you know people like Vanessa's boss, people who like to rain on every parade? Do you know people who often make comments like these?

"It's no use trying."

"You can give it a shot, but you'll never make it."

"We tried that before, and it didn't work."

"It can't happen."

"It's not possible."

"There's no way."

If so, then you know some Wet Blankets.

Wet Blankets treat the possibility of a happy ending with distaste and mild contempt. A free trip to Tahiti means only jet lag and mosquito bites.

Accomplished Wet Blankets can burst any celebratory balloon. "The wedding was so beautiful; such a shame the groom couldn't have lost a few pounds for the occasion." "Congratulations on your new promotion. But you've still got an awful lot of the ladder to climb, don't you?" "The new sanctuary looks wonderful. Of course, we'll probably never grow enough to fill it or pay for it!" Deflating joy, tarnishing triumphs— that's what Wet Blankets do best.

We can even find Wet Blankets in some of the biblical stories. The Pharisees in John's story of the blind man's healing are Wet Blankets (John 9). Instead of rejoicing with the man at the miracle of his regained sight, they pester the man and try to discredit Jesus as a person who does not keep the Law. And, of course, today's church is not immune to Wet Blankets either. There are plenty of modern-day Pharisees who love to find spiritual, theological, and moral "gotchas" to flaunt at others. It's the way of Wet Blankets.

> **A pessimist is one who feels bad when he feels good for fear he'll feel worse when he feels better.** Anonymous

Marshall Shelley, author of *Well-Intentioned Dragons*, says these people have a motto: "Nothing ventured, nothing lost." Add to that "If it ain't broke, don't fix it," and you have the basic attitude of Wet Blankets. These are the people who told the Wright brothers, "If people were meant to fly, God would have given them wings."

As a writer, I have encountered my fair share of Wet Blankets and have a shoe box full of rejection letters from editors and publishers to prove it. As a professor, I have seen dozens of competent students suffer under the weight of Wet Blankets who shoot down their dreams and assault their aspirations. As a psychologist I have heard countless stories from good people who gave in to the negativism of Wet Blankets at work until they had internalized every pessimistic message to the point of becoming depressed.

Thankfully, I have also seen plenty of these same people learn to cope with Wet Blankets' negative messages and rise to unimagined heights. Their secret? We'll get to that in a moment. But first, let's begin with the traits that make Wet Blankets who they are.

THE ANATOMY OF A WET BLANKET

Wet Blankets are automatically negative about whatever makes you excited. If you get a raise, they don't think it's enough. If you win a contest, they are disappointed with the prize. If you accomplish a goal, they don't acknowledge it. The Wet Blankets' negative nature, however, is made up of several specific traits. Wet Blankets are cynical, pessimistic, discounting, deflating, faultfinding, melancholy, stagnant, rejecting, and contaminating.

Cynical

Harry Emerson Fosdick, an influential minister in the early part of the twentieth century, made an interesting observation: "Watch what people are cynical about, and one can often discover what they lack." That is certainly true of Wet Blankets. Cynicism courses through their veins, and while it is sometimes disguised as thoughtful contemplation, it is always a cheap barb to attack in the other person the qualities they themselves lack.

Pessimistic

Wet Blankets suffer from pretraumatic stress syndrome—a tendency to believe that because everything is going so well, disaster must certainly be just around the corner. You will have difficulty finding people more pessimistic than Wet Blankets.

Discounting

"Sure, you made it this time, but let's see if you can do it when it really counts," a track coach said to a young athlete who was working desperately to beat her record in the high jump. The high school student was practicing for an upcoming meet and had just jumped better than she had ever done before. Still, the coach discounted it because it wasn't in the actual meet. That's customary for Wet Blankets. They reject positive experiences by insisting they don't count.

Deflating

Ever had an emotional high from an inspirational message? Have you ever received good news that was beyond your imagining? Or have you ever dreamed a dream you couldn't contain? If so, don't tell Wet Blankets. They will burst your bubble and snuff out your excitement before you know what hit you. Wet Blankets are drawn to good news only to make it not as good as you thought it was.

Faultfinding

Physicists have learned to place defects into perfect crystals to strengthen semiconductors. The imperfections, it turns out, give the crystals their most important quality. Wet Blankets would have a hard time with this practice. They, much like Critics, look at life with a magnifying glass. Scanning the environment for potential flaws, Wet Blankets zero in on minor mistakes and magnify them beyond proportion.

Melancholy

"The typical profile is a person who thinks the past was a failure, the present is miserable and the future looks bleak," says John P. Kildahl, author of *Beyond Negative Thinking*.[1] "Even when something good happens, they think they'll soon pay for it with a host of unavoidable bad events." Wet Blankets are often despondent and sacked with sadness.

Stagnant

Since Wet Blankets see little hope for the future, they find little room for improvement in the present. "Why try?" is the question that reverberates in their mind—so they don't. They douse the flicker of every new idea, including their own, and the result is that Wet Blankets stand stone still, static as a stagnant pond.

Rejecting

I once heard Bruce Feirsten, author of the best-selling book *Real Men Don't Eat Quiche,* interviewed about his experiences as a writer. He said that before that book was accepted for publication, it was turned down twelve times, and one publisher wrote: "I'm sorry, but we can't all be writers. Perhaps you should try to express your talents in another manner." Talk about a Wet Blanket!

Contaminating

Negative-minded people can be poisonous to any home or work environment. Their demeanor usually creates stress and breeds negativism in others. Why? Because they tap the potential for despair in each of us. At some point most of us have felt as if we were victims to forces beyond our control. Because Wet Blankets feel dispirited and defeated, their pessimistic comments can easily arouse resonant feelings in anyone who happens to pay attention to them.

DO YOU KNOW A WET BLANKET?

The following self-test can help you assess whether you are in a high-maintenance relationship with a Wet Blanket. Identify the person or people who have come to your mind as you have read the preceding paragraphs. Circle the *Y* if the statement is true of the person or people about whom you are thinking. Circle the *N* if the statement does not apply to this person or people.

Y   N   If good news is coming, I can count on this person to discount it.

Y   N   "If it ain't broke, don't fix it" characterizes this person.

Y   N   This person is automatically negative about most things.

Y   N   This person often has an attitude of "Why try?"

Y   N   When I feel excited about something, this person can deflate me in a minute.

Y   N   Other people tend to be more negative when this person is near.

Y   N   This person expects the worst.

Y   N   If there is a fault to find, this person will spot it.

Y   N   This person is much more of a pessimist than an optimist.

Y N This person seems to enjoy shooting down another person's idea or proposal.

Y N This person commonly says things like, "It can't happen," "It's not possible," and "There's no way."

Y N This person carries with him or her an air of sadness or *angst*.

Y N This person turns down good ideas.

Y N This person shows little sign of personal growth.

Y N When I am around this person, I tend to be more negative myself.

Scoring: Total the number of Ys you circled. If you circled ten or more Ys, you are certainly in a high-maintenance relationship with a Wet Blanket.

UNDERSTANDING WET BLANKETS

I grew up in an optimistic family. Every idea was worth considering. Every aspiration was worth exploring. But could it have been too optimistic? *Too* optimistic, you ask? Is it possible to be too optimistic? Recent research says so. Julie K. Norem, a psychology professor at Wellesley College, believes that not everyone needs to be optimistic. "To say that pessimism is always bad," says Norem, "is a gross oversimplification. A lot of people out there do very well but are nevertheless quite pessimistic." Norem calls them "defensive pessimists," highly successful people who use anxiety and fear of disaster to help manage their stress and improve their performance.

Some people use pessimism as a defense. They are at their best when they focus on the negative. They are worrywarts who fear failure and have nothing but negativism to protect themselves against anxiety. If they shoot down an idea before it gets off the ground, then they don't have to worry about its possible failure. They need to complain and lower everyone's expectations. They paint the worst-case scenario and then work to keep the worst case from happening, thus harnessing their anxiety as a motivator to do better than expected.

The disciple Thomas may have been a Wet Blanket. In his doubt, Thomas was unable to celebrate Christ's resurrection.

Instead, he demanded proof. His negativism was perhaps his defense mechanism against facing the truth about Christ. When the other disciples told him that they had seen the Lord, he said to them, "Unless I see the nail marks in his hands and put my finger where the nails were, and put my hand into his side, I will not believe it" (John 20:25).

A week later, when Thomas encountered the resurrected Lord, Jesus said to him, "Put your finger here; see my hands. Reach out your hand and put it into my side. Stop doubting and believe" (John 20:27).

Pessimism doesn't make sense to most people, but it does to Wet Blankets, at least to "defensive" Wet Blankets. Other Wet Blankets, perhaps the majority, are simply negative and pessimistic for less "rational" reasons.

Wet Blankets believe that they are pitted against forces beyond their control. Rick, for example, didn't want his work unit to lose office space, but his memos of complaint to headquarters were never even given a reply. *That's it,* Rick reasoned. *I did what I could, and we are stuck.* He gave it a shot and immediately gave in to a helpless state of being victimized. Others might not give up so easily, but for Wet Blankets, these forces are absolute, immutable barriers rather than obstacles to go around, through, or over. Wet Blankets' negativism is not an act. They are truly convinced that they have little power over their own lives. Fate intervenes at every front, never completely within anyone's power to contain. Wet Blankets, with so little belief in anyone's ability to influence change, sit back, complain, and hope fate will deal kindly.

Whatever is true, whatever is noble, whatever is right, whatever is pure, whatever is lovely, whatever is admirable—if anything is excellent or praiseworthy—think about such things.
Philippians 4:8

Negativism is a learned response. Most deep negativism is not inborn— it is learned from parents, teachers, Little League coaches. For instance, some people's parents may have had a gloomy view of life, and that gloominess became contagious. Some people may have even learned to be negative from experiencing a devastating failure—such as not getting in to their college of choice. They may see themselves as damaged goods and believe that no one around them deserves success or happiness.

Could it be that at the core of every Wet Blanket's problem is a basic struggle with low self-esteem? In a vain attempt to feel better about themselves, do Wet Blankets indiscriminately knock down other people's ideas and aspirations?

To find the answers to these questions, Jennifer Crocker and Ian Schwarts asked forty-two college students to complete a questionnaire evaluating their self-esteem.[2] Then, students were arbitrarily divided into two groups, labeled "alphas" and "betas," by the researchers. All the students were asked to indicate their expectations regarding the personality of each person in both groups, rating them on desirable and undesirable characteristics.

What did the alphas have to say about the betas, and vice versa? Despite the fact that these students had never met, their opinions of each other often were colored by their self-esteem.

> A cynic is a man who, when he smells flowers, looks around for a coffin.
> H. L. Mencken

People with high self-esteem rated both groups more favorably than did those whose self-esteem was low. Interestingly, the people with low self-esteem were not at all discriminating: While they showed strong prejudice toward those in the other group, they did not value members of their own group any more highly. Crocker and Schwarts conclude, "Low-self-esteem individuals seem to have a generally negative view of themselves, their own group, other groups, and perhaps the world."

COPING WITH WET BLANKETS

When Roger Bannister was a child, he severely burned his legs in a school accident. He was told by his physician that he would never walk again. As an adult, Bannister became the first person to break the four-minute mile. I'm not sure if Bannister's physician was a charlatan, an incompetent professional, or merely a Wet Blanket, but I do know that we can't believe every piece of bad news we hear. This is foundational to coping with Wet Blankets. Other proven strategies for coping with Wet Blankets include the following.

Face the Wet Blanket Within

In a friend's office hangs a sign that reads, "But we've always done it this way." He says it reminds him how foolish it is to ignore innovation and avoid creative ideas. "It's amazing how many times I hear people say something to that effect in a meeting," he reports. I have to agree. And I have to admit that I have said it myself. Last Sunday, out of reflex, I was driving to a restaurant we often go to after church. Along the way, my wife, Leslie, suggested that we go to a different restaurant. "But we always go to Chinooks on Sunday," I replied. I have a feeling that I'm not alone. Don't tell me you have never pooh-poohed someone's plan or idea. Everyone, at some point, has fallen in line with the Wet Blanket brigade and has said, "It will never work." After all, it doesn't take much effort to lack vision. Negativism is easy. When you understand this part of yourself, you will better understand the Wet Blankets in your life.

> **All the days of the oppressed are wretched, but the cheerful heart has a continual feast.**
> Proverbs 15:15

Guard against Infection

Warning: The Wet Blanket virus is highly contagious. Just like the flu, negativism can unwittingly be transmitted. When people honk insistently on the highway, does your ire rise to match theirs? No word has been spoken, but if you are like most people, you have caught the drivers' negativity. Negativity isn't something anybody would *want* to catch. Why, then, do we? One reason is that many of us are so attuned to our own emotions that we easily pick up on others' emotions. If we're open, we're open: Both positive and negative stuff flows in. And if we try to filter out the latter, the former gets blocked too. So when we are around a negative person, we become negative too. We cut down other people's ideas and make cynical statements. Once we are infected with negativism, it becomes a natural way of relating. It becomes our membership dues to acceptance, and we often pay it without even being aware of it. We must learn to be objective and observe Wet Blankets' feel-

> **A cynic can chill and dishearten with a single word.**
> Ralph Waldo Emerson

ings without getting infected by them. The apostle Paul gives us the best protection against negativism when he says, "Do not conform any longer to the pattern of this world, but be transformed by the renewing of your mind" (Rom. 12:2).

Differentiate between Critical Thinking and Negativism

Not all negative expressions, however, are a result of negativism. We need to learn to differentiate true negativism from critical thinking. When a person says, "Only five percent of all applicants are accepted," that person may be offering a valuable analysis rather than dropping a wet blanket on your idea. Critical thinkers identify possible disasters and can help you plan ways to evade, overcome, or minimize them. In practice, it is fairly easy to tell the two apart. In response to a statement such as "But if we submit an application, it will mean sacrificing some other project," the critical thinker will say, "That's a good point, but we may be able to find some way around that problem" or "Maybe we could manage with one less project." Wet Blankets would hear the same statement and reply, "You're right. There's nothing we can do."

Cheer up, the worst is yet to come.
Philander Johnson

Monitor Your Inner Voice

If you live or work with Wet Blankets, you have almost certainly had your self-confidence taken down a few notches. After hearing so many negative messages, it is only natural to begin to believe them. In order to keep from falling further and to build up your self-confidence, you need to pay attention to your self-talk. What mental tape do you play when you make a mistake? What do you hear in your head when you don't reach your goal?

Do everything without complaining or arguing.
Philippians 2:14

If Wet Blankets have gotten to you, the messages are probably negative: "I'll never succeed." If you are not aware of the messages you give yourself, carry around a notepad and record your inner voice. Jot down what goes through your mind when you have a new idea or don't follow through on a goal you already have set. If you find that Wet Blankets have had a bigger impact than you thought, it's not too late. Simply continue to monitor your messages and begin to replace them with realistic messages. Don't mistake this for positive thinking or happy affirmations or, even worse, self-delusion. The point is not to tell yourself you can be a world-class artist if you can't draw a straight line. The point is to correct flawed, overgeneralized thinking such as "I can't do anything right." Remember that self-talk—positive and negative—has a way of becoming self-fulfilling prophecy. That's why it's so important to monitor your negative messages and counter negativism with realism.

Have a Comeback

Just as you need to counter negative self-talk with realistic positive messages, you also need to learn to come back at Wet Blankets with an expression of your own optimism. If Wet Blankets tell you that something won't work, give an example of a time when it did work. If you can think of a similar example of a past success, a statement such as "I still have faith that we haven't tried everything" is better than nothing. Stating your positive perspective shores up your own commitment, and it may tap the internal balance in Wet Blankets toward a more positive outlook.

> **It takes a clever man to turn cynic and a wise man to be clever enough not to.**
> **Fannie Hurst**

Combat Irrational Thinking

I sometimes use a riddle popularized by Abraham Lincoln in my therapy sessions to demonstrate the importance of combating irrational thinking: "If you call a dog's tail a leg, how many legs does a dog have?" I give the answer to my patients in a sealed envelope to take home, and I request that they give the riddle a great deal of thought. Only after deriving a satisfactory answer are they to open the envelope. And almost invariably, my patients end up comparing their answer of "five legs" to Lincoln's: "A dog continues to have four legs. Calling a dog's tail a leg does not make it so." For the most part, Wet Blankets are no more in touch with reality than are pie-in-the-sky optimists. And remembering this fact can keep you from using the kind of logic Lincoln was trying to dispel. The point is to remember that the Wet Blankets' thinking is not based on reality, so don't give it undue attention.

Keep Keeping On

One of the saddest aspects of living or working with Wet Blankets is that they may convince you to give up your dreams. After hearing their negative sermons, you may begin to believe them and let go of your aspirations and goals. If you are having difficulty holding on to your dreams, fight the temptation and prove the Wet Blankets wrong. Some years ago, as a new professor, I went into my dean's office with an idea to raise $150,000 to help students on our campus prepare for lifelong marriage. Within the first fifteen minutes of our meeting, he said, "Things like that don't work on this campus," and sent me on my way. I was tempted to give up and move on. But I didn't. I talked with other colleagues and students and became all the more convinced of the need. A year later, that money came in, and the program ("Saving Your Marriage Before It Starts") has been running for years. That's one example of millions of ideas that were once targets of Wet Blankets. Ask anyone who is making a dream a reality, and you are guaranteed to hear stories of the Wet Blankets who tried to stop them. So, do you get temporarily discouraged? Fine. But don't give up.

> **Skepticism is slow suicide.**
> Ralph Waldo Emerson

Laugh the Wet Blanket Dry

Proverbs 17:22 says, "A cheerful heart is good medicine." That is so true, but humor can be risky. What is appealing to some is appalling to others. In a survey of over fourteen thousand *Psychology Today* readers who rated thirty jokes, the findings were unequivocal. "Every single joke," it was reported, "had a substantial number of fans who rated it 'very funny,' while another group dismissed it as 'not at all funny.'"[3] Apparently our funny bones are located in different places. But when humor is used appropriately, it can be a great strategy for defusing the sting of Wet Blankets' cynicism because it releases stress. At one point during the Cuban missile crisis, Soviet and American negotiators became deadlocked. They sat in silence until one of the Russians told a riddle: "What is the difference between capitalism and communism?" The answer? "In capitalism, people exploit people. In communism, it's the other way around." Humor relieves stress, and if you can find humor when living or working with Wet Blankets, you will deflect their negativism. "If you can find humor in anything," according to Bill Cosby, "you can survive it." Researchers agree. Studies reveal that people who have a strong sense of humor are less likely to experience depression and other forms of mood disturbance.

Don't Let Wet Blankets Determine Your Mood

When Thomas Jefferson included "the pursuit of happiness" among our inalienable rights, he pinpointed an idea that is important for all of us wanting to live with inward joy: People will interfere with our inalienable right to be happy if we allow them to. I walked with a friend to the newsstand the other night, and he bought a paper, thanking the owner politely. The owner, however, did not even acknowledge it. When I made a comment about the guy's sullenness, my friend shrugged and said, "Oh, he's that way every night." When I asked why my friend continued to be so polite, he replied,

> My pessimism goes to the point of suspecting the sincerity of the pessimists.
> Edmond Rostand

"Why should I let him determine how I'm going to act?" What an insight! But what really impressed me was that my friend was practicing it. To know that other people don't control our moods is one thing; but to live out this belief is quite another thing. So practice this lesson with Wet Blankets every chance you get, and soon it will become habit.

Know Where to Go (and Not to Go) for Help

I love the story of the man who consulted with his doctor about a problem. After listening to the man, the doctor said, "I'm sure I have the answer to your problem." The man answered, "I certainly hope so, Doctor. I should have come to you long ago." The doctor asked, "Where did you go before?" "I went to the pharmacist," the man offered. The doctor snidely remarked, "What kind of foolish advice did he give you?" The man responded, "He told me to come see you!" Like this doctor, Wet Blankets are often consulted for advice. For whatever reason —their training, experience, position—they are sometimes seen as the people to be consulted. But

Wet Blankets should be the last people anyone consults for advice unless they want to be discouraged. Instead, seek wisdom and guidance from people who are known for their optimistic spirit and reality-based perspectives. These are the people who will give wings to your ideas.

Don't Hold Out for Transformation

Trying to change Wet Blankets' negativism is often a no-win battle. One of this country's most effective ministers gave me a tour of the beautiful grounds surrounding his tremendous church. Today it is an expanding church with thousands of members, but some years ago it started with a handful of people on the outskirts of town. He told me how God had given him a vision for helping people internalize positive principles from Scripture and how he had worked for months to get his message across to his small congregation. But, like a thorn

A cynic is just a man who found out when he was ten that there wasn't any Santa Claus, and he's still upset. J. G. Cozzens

in his side, several people who didn't like his style or his message spent much of their energy griping and complaining. They eventually tried to get him to leave. "Les," this pastor said as he paused in his story to look me in the face, "the best thing that ever happened to this church was when that group of negative people decided I wasn't leaving, and they left instead." Some negative people are bound and determined to be negative. Accepting this fact can help us decide either to hang in there with all their negativism or to cut bait and move on.

CROSS-REFERENCE

For more information related to Wet Blankets, see these other high-maintenance relationships: the Cold Shoulder, the Gossip, the Critic, and the Steamroller.

5

THE STEAMROLLER

Blindly Insensitive to Others

E.H

STAN has all the subtlety of a freight train. He is full of bluster and bravado, whether he is at home or at the office. And his lack of tact, coupled with clumsy attempts at communication, frequently alienate him from coworkers and his own family. Stan will blurt out critical comments, never knowing the damage he is doing to people's feelings: "What's wrong with your hair?" "You're out in left field again; get back to the main issue," or "You are telling me this as if I were actually interested."

Ever heard statements like these? Do you know people like Stan, people with the interpersonal skills of a Neanderthal? Do you know people who step on other people's toes and don't seem to know it? If so, then you know some Steamrollers. Hurting people's feelings seems to be their *modus operandi,* and they do it quite innocently. They simply roll through life, flattening everyone and anyone with their insensitivity. It's enough to make even the thick-skinned person cringe.

My friend Joan works for a Steamroller. When Joan turned in a report, her boss took one look at it and said, "The accountant hated that format last time, and you used it again!" Joan was too shaken to respond. Everyone in Joan's office fears the boss. He'll say anything, however hurtful, and he pays little attention to the emotional consequences. Joan and her coworkers do everything they can to avoid this man's wrath, but as he has said more than once in his staff meetings: "We are not in this company to test the waters. We are in this company to make waves."

Never contend with one that is foolish, proud, positive, testy, or with a superior or a clown, in matters of argument. Thomas Fuller

That's typical talk for Steamrollers. They aren't afraid to make waves, and they don't mind causing a few fireworks either. I know someone who says Steamrollers speak with an exclamation point instead of a period at the end of their sentences. Steamrollers are verbal terrorists who put everyone on red alert.

When Steamrollers want your opinion, they give it to you. And if you don't go along with their wishes, look out! Their motto is "My way or the highway."

As the survey I mentioned in chapter 1 indicated, many people interact daily with Steamrollers. Most people indicated it was the fourth-most-difficult kind of high-maintenance relationship they faced. If you know Steamrollers— or even if you live with some— don't despair. While you will not change their personality in "three easy steps," you can learn to manage this high-maintenance relationship and avoid getting run over. As always, the way to improvement begins by better understanding who Steamrollers really are.

THE ANATOMY OF A STEAMROLLER

Steamrollers may be chief executive officers who are accustomed to calling the shots all day at the office and can't relinquish control at home. Or they may work in an environment as underlings, and bullying may be the only way to get things done. Or maybe Steamrollers are simply blind to everyone else's feelings and blurt out remarks without a clue. Whatever the status or the reason, most Steamrollers have the following traits in common. They are arrogant, independent, blaming, condescending, political, discarding, blustering, stubborn, and rude.

Arrogant

"I'm in trouble because I'm normal and slightly arrogant," said professional boxer Mike Tyson in a recent interview. "A lot of people don't like themselves, and I happen to be totally in love with myself." By all appearances, Steamrollers seem to be in love with themselves too. Just as peacocks raise their tail feathers to scare off attackers, Steamrollers often disguise weakness with an air of arrogance, a know-it-all attitude that has answers for everything.

Independent

Steamrollers exude a feeling of power, personal authority, and independence. They seem to need other people very little, if at all. They leave little room for anyone else's judgments, creativity, or resourcefulness. They see little need to listen to anyone else's facts or knowledge. Steamrollers, if you hadn't noticed, already know the best way to proceed.

Blaming

In spite of their independent spirit, Steamrollers often avoid responsibility when things go wrong by shifting the blame. The fault lies with incompetents (like you and me) who are responsible for messing things up. So while Steamrollers may have come up with an idea and set the wheels in motion for implementing it, they will go to great lengths to point the finger at somebody else if it fails.

Condescending

Since Steamrollers perceive that they are always right, they leave others feeling like objects of condescension. "You really should have known better than to do that," they will say. Or, "I've told you before that you look foolish when you don't take my advice." And while these kinds of statements are often made without conscious malice, they still leave others feeling like children being scolded by their teacher.

Political

For Steamrollers, every day is an engagement in a larger-than-life chess game in which they play to win. They know who has the power and who holds the purse strings. Some Steamrollers may even employ situational ethics, manipulate people for their personal gain, and say and do whatever will get them ahead. Steamrollers often use people for their own self-aggrandizement.

Discarding

Relating to a Steamroller is like riding a bicycle— if you don't pedal forward, you'll fall off. I have met plenty of people who don't last in their jobs because a Steamroller boss had little time for mentoring or watching over a new employee. Steamrollers are on the move, and if you don't get on board quickly, they will run right over you.

Blustering

Steamrollers can intrude on a relatively peaceful scene with the insistence of a stuck horn. You don't have to be Dick Tracy to detect Steamrollers. They give themselves away by their loud, obnoxious, abrasive, and boisterous style. When they enter your presence, the atmospheric conditions change.

Stubborn

Steamrollers are so determined to get their own way that they write their diary in advance. And once they have their sights set on a particular goal, there is no arguing them out of it. Compromise is unspeakable to Steamrollers. They are right, and everyone else is wrong. Period. End of discussion. Seventeenth-century clergyman Henry Ward Beecher must have had Steamrollers in mind when he said, "The difference between perseverance and obstinacy is that one comes from a strong will, and the other from a strong won't."

Rude

There is no denying it. Steamrollers can be rude. Without flinching they can make a remark that no other civilized person would even whisper. "You really have a big nose, don't you?" "I see you're not the world's greatest driver." Or, "You'll never attract a date if you blab this much all the time."

DO YOU KNOW A STEAMROLLER?

The following self-test can help you assess whether you are in a high-maintenance relationship with a Steamroller. Identify the person or people who have come to your mind as you have read the preceding paragraphs. Circle the *Y* if the statement is true of the person or people about whom you are thinking. Circle the *N* if the statement does not apply to this person or people.

Y N   I often feel flattened by this person's insensitivity.

Y N   Everyone knows when this blustering person enters the room.

Y N   This person is undeniably and fiercely independent.

Y N   This person makes rude comments without even realizing it.

Y N   This person is stubborn and persistent, no matter what the obstacle.

Y N   I feel that if this person doesn't like me, he or she will drop me like a hot potato.

Y N   This person often comes across as quite arrogant.

Y N   This person is very conscious of who holds the power and what it will take to get the powerful person on his or her side.

Y N   Arguing with this person is always a bad idea.

Y N   This person does not recognize the interpersonal damage he or she causes.

Y N   This person is closed-minded and not interested in other people's input.

Y N   I often feel like a child when this person speaks to me in a condescending tone.

Y N   Most of the time this person isn't even aware of how he or she makes other people feel.

Y N   People often do everything they can to please this person because he or she is intimidating.

Y N   This person will blurt out rude comments that sometimes make me wince.

Scoring: Total the number of Ys you circled. If you circled ten or more Ys, you are certainly in a high-maintenance relationship with a Steamroller.

UNDERSTANDING STEAMROLLERS

Frank, a thirty-six-year-old father of two, is married to a very understanding woman. For most of their twelve-year marriage, Rachel has endured Frank's pushy, intimidating, and sometimes downright rude style of interacting. Frank's demeaning style and self-imposed kingship has been the source of endless arguments and frustration. But Rachel has stood by her commitment to her steamrolling husband—partly out of conviction and mostly because she understands why he does what he does.

Frank was raised in a small town on the East Coast. He was a gifted child who felt misunderstood and ridiculed for his brilliance. He spent much of his childhood alone, brooding and feeling different. He felt as if his parents didn't understand him. He spent a lot of time explaining himself to his teachers. He labored through the teasing of his peers, and he found solace in the company of animals. He thought for years that he might become a veterinarian, but his education took him into administration.

The gem cannot be polished without friction, nor man perfected without trials.
Chinese proverb

Early on, Frank decided that the world was a hostile place. He decided that in order to survive, he had to take care of himself and guard himself against a cruel world. As an adult, Frank is over six feet tall and an imposing figure. But on the inside, he is very much a ten-year-old boy wanting to be accepted but not willing to take the necessary risks. He guards himself at an unconscious level by looking out for "number one" and disregarding others' emotions.

Not all Steamrollers grew up in the kind of environment Frank did. But you can be assured that *most Steamrollers have some unconscious emotional pain that has never been resolved.* The result is a thick layer of protective insulation that suffocates emotional sensitivity. Being hard-hitting and even verbally abusive guards Steamrollers against potential pain. It is a way of being visibly protective (like the peacock who spreads its feathers to appear larger) without being withdrawn (like the turtle). In a sense, Steamrollers make a choice—sometimes conscious, other times unconscious—to respond to life's unfairness not as Martyrs, who take life lying down, but as fighters who need to bully their way out of life's pain. It is a fundamental approach to life, usually so deeply ingrained that it absorbs the Steamroller's personality.

As a part of this personality package, *Steamrollers avoid vulnerable involvement with others.* Their certainty that their own theories, facts, and procedures are correct makes them gruff to others, but it also makes Steamrollers feel the world is more predictable and safe.

Steamrollers avoid risk. In his novel *The Fall,* Albert Camus tells of a man in Amsterdam who spends most of his life sitting in a bar: "I never cross a bridge at night. . . . Suppose, after all, that someone should jump in the water. One of two things —either you do likewise to fish him out, and in cold weather, you run a great risk! Or you forsake him there and suppressed dives sometimes leave one strangely aching." Camus' character is afraid. But he's not afraid of crossing bridges or diving into cold water. He is more afraid of getting involved, even by chance, in any situation in which he might have to make a choice, where he might have to take a risk.

> **Remind the people to be subject to rulers and authorities, to be obedient, to be ready to do whatever is good, to slander no one, to be peaceable and considerate, and to show true humility toward all men. Titus 3:1-2**

Steamrollers impose their own order on everything they can. Without intention, they plow through life to avoid more pain, unaware of the pain they are causing others. Why can't they see the damage they do? Because each time Steamrollers chug firmly and methodically to a planned objective, flattening whatever and whomever stands in the way, they reinforce the security that comes from being self-directing, self-sustaining, and formidable to others.

COPING WITH STEAMROLLERS

Handling Steamrollers requires finesse, strength, and determination. You can't expect to change a hard-core Steamroller. The only thing you can change in this high-maintenance relationship is your approach to it. Here are several effective strategies you can use to make life more manageable with Steamrollers.

Face the Steamroller Within

Of all the high-maintenance relationships in this book, Steamrollers may be the one most difficult for you to empathize with. Most likely you see yourself as a much more sensitive person than Steamrollers. However, be honest. Haven't you ever felt that you wanted to break the if-you-don't-have-anything-nice-to-say rule and blurt out what you are really thinking? When some punk is about to make a costly mistake against your warning, wouldn't you like to say with Clint Eastwood: "Go ahead, make my day"? If not, you are a thoroughly kind person who might border on being a saint. The point is that if you can identify, at least a little, with Steamrollers in your life, you will be better equipped to handle them and show a little compassion.

> **He who establishes his argument by noise and command shows that his reason is weak.**
> Michel de Montaigne

Acknowledge the Difficulty

In work situations where Steamrollers are in charge, they may get away with behavior that would not be accepted in other situations. Like the fable of the emperor's new clothes, people don't want to admit that the emperor is naked and that his new clothes are actually no clothes at all. They're too intimidated, and they don't want to make waves. It's easier just to smile and say the emperor is a great guy than to come out and admit the emperor is deluded. The same is true when it comes to living or working with Steamrollers. People feel intimidated by Steamrollers. However, we do ourselves no favors when we ignore their insensitive ways. Everyone feels Steamrollers' insensitivity. Everyone recognizes it. So when it is appropriate, acknowledge the difficulty of this high-maintenance relationship. Bringing it into the open can help to minimize the stress of denying it.

Find the Good in Steamrollers

Sometimes at work and at home, tough decisions have to be made. This is often where Steamrollers shine. You may not want to admit it, but sometimes Steamrollers' abrasive ways have a positive side. They may cause suffering along the way, but they are decisive, and they get things done. Tell me, how would World War II have been different without a General Patton? The fact is that some companies even go out of their way to hire Steamrollers. "Wild Duck" is IBM jargon for a maverick who causes headaches but also sparks unconventional new ideas on the way to accomplishing a task. It may be hard, but if you can, look for the redeeming characteristics hidden beneath the difficult exterior of the Steamrollers in your life.

Avoid a Power Struggle

You're in the midst of a presentation at a meeting when your boss interrupts with a sneer, "That's a lousy presentation." What do you do? By far, the worst thing you can do with this Steamroller is get into a power struggle in front of everybody. A better approach is to ignore the remark or repeat it in a thoughtful voice— "lousy presentation"—and then move on. You haven't insulted the Steamroller, and people listening know you're in control. This way you maintain your dignity and avoid a humiliating scene. The same holds true if your spouse is a Steamroller and says something snide to you in front of the kids. Avoid a confrontation (at least temporarily) and move on.

> **Fools rush in where angels fear to tread.**
> Alexander Pope

Affirm When You Can

Whenever you can, acknowledge Steamrollers' contributions. Affirm their positive actions. But don't overdo it. Don't fall into the trap of being subservient. Steamrollers tend to like people who think and evaluate for themselves. If you show fear, Steamrollers are all the more likely to run you down. One of the best ways of keeping connected is to request Steamrollers' feedback on a routine basis. It is the only way you can be certain that you are on the right track, at least according to Steamrollers.

Propose Potential Alternatives

When Steamrollers are coming on heavy with an idea you know is not going to work, don't try to convince them that it won't. That is only a challenge to Steamrollers to prove that it will. Instead, you need to get Steamrollers to consider your alternative view while avoiding a direct challenge. For example, you can say something like, "I realize that this probably won't be what we'll end up with, but could we take a minute just to see if there might be anything useful there at all?" Only the most headstrong Steamrollers can resist this humble approach.

Set Your Boundaries

As a kid, I was the ball boy for a soccer team at the college where my father worked. I ran back and forth along the sideline ready to retrieve a ball that went out of bounds. Of course, when it did, the action on the field stopped. The same is true when you learn to set boundaries with Steamrollers. Since your life has neither referees to blow the whistle nor coaches to call a time-out, you become responsible for saying "Foul" and "You are out of bounds" when Steamrollers run you down. You alone manage the game. So set some boundaries with Steamrollers in your life. Set limits on what is acceptable behavior for you. Maybe you need more courtesy when they make a request. Perhaps you want your opinions to be taken more seriously. Decide what you want, be specific, and let Steamrollers know the rules. When they step out-of-bounds, blow the whistle and call a time-out before you resume play. The idea, as the next paragraph makes clear, is not to be bullied.

> **Boldness is a mask for fear, however great.** Lucan

Don't Be Bullied

Monty's three predecessors could not work with their Steamroller boss. Each quit because he couldn't take the insensitive criticisms the boss doled out. Like most Steamrollers, this boss often resorted to intimidation and public ridicule, but Monty wouldn't put up with it. Monty simply ignored these outbursts. But after a meeting in which he was the target, Monty went to his boss privately and told him he had been out of line with him and his coworkers. After this confrontation, Monty's boss came to the next staff meeting and said, "It's been brought to my attention that I may have gone over the line and should apologize. I don't think I did, but if any of you think so, then I do." Monty won a small victory and laid the ground rules for their relationship. A key part of Monty's confrontation, of course, was his calm, rational, and professional manner. He did not attack his boss; he simply stated that he refused to be bullied or to work in an environment where others were too.

When You Lose (and You Will), Do It with Dignity

Recognize that if you live or work with Steamrollers, you will lose some battles. You may not get to choose the restaurant for lunch, the color of the new carpet, the strategy for a presentation, and so on. But when those times occur, you can "lose" in the right way. For starters, you shouldn't expect to get in the last word. This only becomes a challenge to Steamrollers, and you will prolong your agony. Instead, allow Steamrollers to have the last word—but do so on your terms. Say something like, "I am ready and willing to hear your decision, but only when you patiently walk me through your reasoning." This kind of a statement may mean that you give up the battle, but you win back your dignity.

> **The difference between the right word and the almost right word is the difference between lightning and the lightning bug.**
> Mark Twain

Look for an Open Door

As a medical psychologist, I have spent quite a few hours in the intensive-care waiting room observing anguished people, listening to their urgent questions: Will my husband make it? Will my child walk again? A waiting room like this is unlike any other place on earth. People here, total strangers, cannot do enough for each other. No one is rude. The distinctions of race and class melt away. The truck driver loves his wife as much as the high-powered CEO loves his, and everyone understands this. All vanity and pretense vanish, and each person pulls for everyone else. Why? Because it is a time of vulnerability. The good news is that these moments, thankfully, occur not only in hospital waiting rooms. If you live with Steamrollers, you can count on them letting down their guard on occasion—usually after a surprising setback—and that is the time to be fully present. Don't let their hard shell trick you into thinking they don't need you near. And don't give in to the temptation of saying "I told you so." Use this opportunity to tap into their pain (which certainly triggers any pain they may have suffered as children), and do what you can to bring healing. These vulnerable moments, more than any other time, are open doors to potentially kinder, gentler Steamrollers.

CROSS-REFERENCE

For more information related to Steamrollers, see these other high-maintenance relationships: the Backstabber, the Cold Shoulder, the Critic, and the Wet Blanket.

6

THE GOSSIP

*Spreads Rumors and
Leaks Secrets*

"THE Snake that poisons everybody. It topples governments, wrecks marriages, ruins careers, busts reputations, causes heartaches, nightmares, indigestion, spawns suspicion, generates grief, dispatches innocent people to cry in their pillows. Even its name hisses. It's called gossip. Shop gossip. Party gossip. It makes headlines and headaches. Before you repeat a story, ask yourself: Is it true? Is it fair? Is it necessary? If not, shut up." United Technologies, the conglomerate, placed this minilecture in newspapers across the country for no other reason than to make people take a second look at gossip. And with good reason.

Gossips have plagued the earth since people began to talk; they have also been denounced in all generations. The apostle Paul warns about the destructive power of gossip and the condemnation that comes to "gossips and busybodies" who say "things they ought not to" say (1 Tim. 5:13). The Greek chronicler Hesiod, writing at the same time as Homer, declared near the end of *Works and Days:* "Gossip is mischievous, light and easy to raise, but grievous to bear and hard to get rid of. No gossip ever dies away entirely." Shakespeare expressed the right sentiment when he wrote in *Twelfth Night:* "When my tongue blabs, then let mine eyes not see." Lewis Carroll wrote in *Alice's Adventures in Wonderland:* "'If everyone minded their own business,' said the Duchess in a hoarse growl, 'the world would go round a good deal faster than it does.'"

> **None are so fond of secrets as those who do not mean to keep them.**
> Charles Caleb Colton

A reputation is a person's most precious possession. The Bible says, "A good name is more desirable than great riches" (Prov. 22:1). And people who gossip rob us of our good name. When people gossiped about Othello, he was moved to cry: "Reputation, reputation, reputation! O! I have lost my reputation. I have lost the immortal part of myself, and what remains is bestial."

Gossip, no doubt about it, is evil, but it has never been more popular. Today gossip fuels over fifty television talk shows, more than forty newspaper columns, dozens of magazines, and at least three major supermarket tabloids. The illicit goings-on of the rich and famous land on the nightly news and make big headlines more frequently than any serious journalist cares to admit. Gossip about actor Woody Allen's affair with his wife's adopted daughter or gossip about actor Hugh Grant's encounter with a prostitute on Hollywood Boulevard or the royal family's latest faux pas frequently nudge significant news off the front pages of our newspapers. It seems at times we have become a nation of snoops.

But some people take this snooping much more seriously and much further than idle prattle. They are Gossips, people who engage in the over-the-back-fence or at-the-watercooler type of gossip. They are the people who love the latest local rumor, are seemingly incapable of keeping secrets, and are dead set on making our lives more complicated.

THE ANATOMY OF A GOSSIP

Most people have certain stereotypical ideas about gossip and gossipers. Think about gossip and you probably envision housewives gabbing over the clothesline about a neighbor's drinking problem. Or you may think of teenage girls exchanging malicious remarks over the telephone about their classmates. These perceptions, however, are not only sexist; they are wrong. Women are no more likely to gossip than men are. So don't limit this high-maintenance relationship to one gender. You may be surprised to find Gossips in the most unlikely places. Here are some of the most common traits of Gossips: talkative, pseudosecretive, negative, intrusive, deceitful, vicious, superficial, and self-righteous.

Talkative

Writer William Wilderson once said the anatomy of any organization includes different kinds of "bones": Wishbones who wish someone else would do the work, Knucklebones who knock what everyone else does, Backbones who actually do the work, and Jawbones who talk incessantly but do little else. Gossips fall into this last category. They often chatter nonstop and drive the people around them crazy. They prattle on about the latest hot news, wanting to cover the same ground again and again.

Pseudosecretive

Gossips start a lot of sentences with: "You have to promise you won't tell Brenda I told you this because she made me swear not to tell anyone. . . ." It sounds very confidential. But then why are they telling you the secret? You see, Gossips appear to be keeping a secret, but they are doing just the opposite: They are giving away the secret to whomever will listen. It should come as no surprise that if they're telling Brenda's secrets, they're telling yours too.

Negative

When I visited recently in a beautifully appointed home, I saw on the sofa an embroidered pillow with this startling message: "If you haven't got anything good to say about anyone, come and sit by me." Gossips love negative news about anyone. They move like magnets toward the latest personal tragedy in someone's life. It is almost as if they are sifting out the good to be sure to recognize the bad.

Intrusive

They say that hell for Gossips is a place where people are forced to mind their own business. Have you ever noticed how difficult it is for Gossips to do just that? In an almost compulsive fashion, they wheedle their way into private places, trying to discover the secrets that aren't ready to be told. They tread fearlessly to find out someone's heartache or latest embarrassment. Gossips, in plain language, are nosy.

Deceitful

Did you know that the average person tells about thirteen lies per week? Paul Ekman, professor of psychology at the University of California Medical School and author of *Telling Lies,* has been studying lies for twenty years. His research has revealed that we don't even realize when we're lying. Gossips often tell "spontaneous" lies just for fun. But the damage done by these lies is far from fun.

Vicious

British novelist George Meredith once said, "A gossip is a beast of prey who does not even wait for the death of his victim." Gossiping is a behind-the-back blood sport of ruining people's reputation. "For what do we live," asked Mr. Bennett in Jane Austen's novel *Pride and Prejudice,* "but to make sport for our neighbors and to laugh at them in turn?" Hard-core Gossips enjoy seeing someone's reputation crumble. They might laugh as they tell you how your friend threw a lamp at her husband's head and cut his forehead. They take pleasure in chipping away at one's character or driving division between people. As Proverbs 16:28 says, "A perverse man stirs up dissension, and a gossip separates close friends."

Superficial

Tim Stafford, author of *That's Not What I Meant,* calls gossip "conversational junk food." I couldn't agree more. Gossips have little depth of character. They rely on superficial hearsay to form the heart of their conversations. "Gossip is the sort of smoke that comes from the dirty tobacco pipes of those who diffuse it," according to English novelist George Eliot. "It proves nothing but the bad taste of the smoker."

Self-Righteous

The evil nature of gossip is illustrated by the fact that tart-tongued Gossips get upset at the prospect of others gossiping about them. "I find that when I am gossiping about my friends, as well as my enemies, I am deeply conscious of performing a social duty," notes anthropologist Max Gluckman with tongue in cheek. "But when I hear they gossip about me, I am rightfully filled with righteous indignation."

DO YOU KNOW A GOSSIP?

The following self-test can help you assess whether you are in a high-maintenance relationship with a Gossip. Identify the person or people who have come to your mind as you have read the preceding paragraphs. Circle the *Y* if the statement is true of the person or people about whom you are thinking. Circle the *N* if the statement does not apply to this person or people.

Y N   This person seems to "let the cat out of the bag" far too frequently.

Y N   This person enjoys telling me about someone else's misfortunes.

Y N   This person has little going on in his or her own life but knows a lot about what's going on in everyone else's.

Y N   The term *meddling* often describes this person.

Y N   I know of people who have been deeply hurt by this person's stories about them.

Y N   This person belittles others.

Y N   This person snoops out information but doesn't keep secrets.

Y N   This person loves to talk about everybody but himself or herself.

Y N   I can point to specific situations in which this person embellished a story in ways that were flagrantly not true.

Y N   Most people would agree that this person is not trust-worthy.

Y N   This person seems to comb through the flowers of a person's life to find the weeds.

Y   N   This person acts secretive but is often telling a secret.

Y   N   Other people look to this person for the inside scoop.

Y   N   This person can become very self-righteous if someone else gossips about him or her.

Y   N   When I am with this person, I sometimes feel as if he or she is inappropriately prying into areas of my life.

Scoring: Total the number of Ys you circled. If you circled ten or more Ys, you are certainly in a high-maintenance relationship with a Gossip.

UNDERSTANDING GOSSIPS

In its broadest sense, gossip can be defined as personal information without corroboration. But for dedicated Gossips, it is more. Behind serious gossip is unkind motivation. Recently I saw in a Jewish publication an advertisement dominated by a drawing of a very stern-looking, bearded rabbi of the nineteenth century, the Chofetz Chaim, who wrote a book about gossip, *Guard Your Tongue.* At the bottom of the page was a "hot line" number to call anonymously if you had information about someone's potential marriage, business partner, or whatever. A rabbi at the other end would tell you whether your gossip was important enough to pass along. If not, you would be counseled to guard your tongue. In other words, the service was making a distinction between private information that can bring about good and private information for gossip's sake. But for Gossips, there is no difference. Rarely is their gossip inspired by a consideration to save an innocent bride from a brutish bridegroom. Often their gossip is fueled by malice or a warped sense of pleasure in someone else's discomfort.

Why? Why would Gossips be so predisposed? Several reasons come to mind. Gossips want to be "in the know," to have the inside scoop. Everyone enjoys knowing information that most people aren't privy to, but Gossips make it their job. They feel special if they are among the privileged few who know why a person at work is divorcing her husband or why a friend at church hasn't spoken to his sister in years.

Experts who have studied gossip believe we all indulge in a little gossip from time to time because talking about others is a part of our

behavioral makeup, ingrained in us both socially and psychologically. "If a group of friends or coworkers are engaged in a gabfest, you
naturally want to join in," says Dr. Jack Levine, a sociology professor
at Northeastern University and author of *Gossip: The Inside Scoop.* But
while most of us understand this superficial way of
passing time, Gossips take their work much more
seriously. For them *gossip serves as the key to social
acceptance* and thus prevents them from keeping the
simplest of secrets. Gossips spill the beans, in other
words, to create a bond, a friendship through secrets. They gain
intimacy with one person by trading the secrets of another. Gossips
blab away, convinced that telling you somebody's very personal
secret will endear them to you.

Without wood a fire goes out; without gossip a quarrel dies down. Proverbs 26:20

It's that need to feel accepted that encourages Gossips at times
to embellish stories about people. In a university experiment
conducted by Professor Levin, gossip about a campus wedding
was spread among the student body of a large university. The
wedding was fictitious; it never happened. Yet 12 percent of the
students questioned said they had attended the wedding. Some of
them even went so far as to describe the wedding gown. To be in
the know helps Gossips feel that they will be accepted.

*Another reason Gossips love a juicy piece of news is that it tends to
normalize their life.* If their marriage is falling apart, Gossips want
to know about everyone else who is having marital struggles. It
makes them feel better to know they are not alone. So they
compare themselves to other people in the hope that they will find
that the other people are struggling with something much worse
than they are. And when Gossips find someone struggling with
drug use or alcoholism, they feel better. If they hear of someone
who is confused about sexual preference, they feel better. If they
discover a colleague has a threatening illness or unwieldy children,
they feel better. Gossips feel more confident if they can find other
people who are doing worse than they are.

*A third reason people gossip is that they find it a way to influence or
change the behavior of others without confronting them directly and appear-
ing accusatory or risking hurt feelings.* This reason was confirmed in a
study conducted among sorority women at Temple University in

Philadelphia.[1] For example, if Jennifer doesn't like to be around people who drink, she might gossip to her friends about how she dislikes being around Kathie because she drinks. That way, anyone who listened to the gossip gets the message— don't drink around Jennifer— without being confronted directly. And, eventually, Kathie and other drinkers may hear the gossip through the grapevine and refrain from drinking in Jennifer's presence.

Sometimes Gossips can't keep a secret because they simply don't understand why it's a secret. If you ask Pamela not to tell anyone that your two-and-a-half-year-old isn't potty-trained, she might think, *What's the big deal?* If the topic comes up with somebody else, Gossips may not think twice about mentioning your private information.

Some Gossips tell secrets to gain power. Gossiping often causes pain, and out of that pain Gossips feel more powerful, if only for a fleeting moment. Rumors travel, intensifying as they circulate, and inevitably fly back to the subject to provoke anguish, bitterness, and hatred. Cheap prattle, particularly that preceded by "don't tell a soul," takes on a life of its own, wrecking other lives in its path. That doesn't seem to bother many Gossips. They only know that for the moment, they feel a little stronger.

COPING WITH GOSSIPS

The private lives of the rich and famous are the fodder for what writer Lance Morrow in *Time* magazine calls *macrogossip*, the international-class gossip that is shared just between you, me, and twenty million other readers. Insecure and attention-starved Gossips would hardly be a bother if they stuck to such far-removed topics as celebrity escapades. Unfortunately their poison usually hits much closer to home, on the level of microgossip. The good news is that you don't have to put up with it. Try these effective strategies for deflecting rumors and protecting yourself from high-maintenance Gossips.

Recognize the Gossip Within

Fess up. In the supermarket line, when no one you know is around, you speed-read the *National Enquirer* and hope the cashier is even slower than usual. You would never, of course, actually buy the tabloid paper, but something within you enjoys a tidbit of gossip now and then. What harm is there in knowing the Hollywood rumors about who is dating and divorcing whom and what celebrities are having plastic surgery? Maybe no harm is done there, but what about your desire to get the scoop on people in your office? Does a part of you want to hear the scandals about the people in your life? Honestly, the temptation to participate in gossip is strong. Why? Gossip gives us power. We can achieve instant power by gossiping about someone. However, you may recognize

> Of every ten persons who talk about you, nine will say something bad, and the tenth will say something good in a bad way.
> Antoine Rivarol

something that Gossips do not: The power vanishes as swiftly as it came. As soon as the gossip is uttered, the power has vanished. You can begin to manage high-maintenance Gossips by recognizing that you also are sometimes tempted to gossip.

Don't Just Sit There, Say Something

You are at the watercooler at work and step into a seemingly innocent conversation with a colleague: "Ron is dumber than a box of rocks. He can't tell the time of day in a room full of clocks. You know, I heard he was hired because his old man pulled some strings. I don't think he even has a college education." What do you do? It is gossip, no denying that. After all, you didn't know Ron's dad was a bigwig, and you have often wondered how Ron got his job. Could it be true? You ponder it. But do you listen for more gossip, or do you clarify your colleague's content? The truth is, saying nothing and listening eagerly for more makes you just as guilty as Gossips. It proves the seldom-understood adage: "The sins of omission are far greater than the sins of commission." Speaking up, clarifying the source of information, and finding the facts can keep misinformation from spreading like wildfire. You can say something like, "Are you sure you have your facts straight, or is it just something you are wondering?" The point is to take a hard view of unsubstantiated claims; otherwise you are giving tacit approval to Gossips. A study by Indiana University sociologist Donna Eder shows that how a person reacts to gossip helps decide the fate of the subject. For three years, Eder listened in on the conversations of seventy-nine girls. Eder found that gossip damage is diminished if someone on the receiving end of the information sticks up for or defends the person in question. On the other hand, if the person joins in on the gossip, a character assassination often results.[2] As Proverbs 26:20 says, "Without wood a fire goes out; without gossip a quarrel dies down."

Lay Off the Guilt Trip

What would be your immediate response if a Gossip burst into your office to tell you about Kevin, the new trainee? "All morning our little genius has been calling clients and giving them the wrong information about our new products. When I found out, I nearly hit the ceiling!" Your colleague goes on to tell you the terrible damage it could have caused if he had not caught the error. "Besides, I think the real problem here," he states, "is that Kevin is smoking pot. He has to be doing something funny to make a mistake like that." At this point, you realize your colleague, a Gossip, is simply dreaming up information without the facts.

> A gossip usually makes a mountain out of a molehill by adding some dirt.

What do you do? The best alternative is to run the rumor into a dead end without condemning your colleague. You could say something like, "Good thing you caught it. It is unfortunate that it happened. I have worked on only one job with Kevin, and he is the one who spotted an error I was making. He kept me from looking pretty foolish." A statement like this doesn't condemn Gossips, and it doesn't start an argument. By your calm example, you are clearly saying, "I accept what you saw; therefore I expect that you accept what I saw." This way Gossips can retain some self-respect. The point is that you cannot score a dramatic victory with Gossips by verbal jousting. As soon as an argument ignites, Gossips will be concocting their own rumors about you. It simply adds fuel to the flames. So avoid the preachy, public correction of Gossips.

Have a Parachute Plan

Let's face it. Sometimes it's not easy to be calm and cool with Gossips. Sometimes it's not easy to be benevolent. What can you do when you are just not in the mood for altruistic alchemy? If you can't redirect a gossipy conversation without taking Gossips on a guilt trip, it is time for plan B: Say nothing and keep on walking. Sometimes simply refusing to take part in garbage is better than uttering insipid words that stick in your throat. It may be tough, but sometimes we need to realize that we can't save the world, let alone Gossips. Working or living with Gossips is sometimes like trying to cover all the graffiti painted in public rest rooms. It is an impossible task. You can't cut off every rumor at the pass.

Assess Your Corporate Climate

If your primary encounters with Gossips are in the work setting, consider the atmosphere of your workplace. Is your office a rumor mill? Does it breed suspicion and scandal? If so, it reveals not just a breach in the confidence of Gossips but a deeper flaw in the department and the company. In *From Here to Eternity* James Jones accurately described an Army company as "a single personality formed by many soldiers." This observation is true of any organization. If the superiors are intrusive and vicious, their attitudes will determine the corporate culture, and it may be next to impossible to rid yourself of rumors at work. I have a friend, Laura Jones, who works as a news anchor for a major television network in Chicago. She told me that her cutthroat industry is rife with rumors and gossip. "Once I understood that the gossip was endemic and not just an issue for me, I was better able to cope," she told me. "I don't like it, but I choose to put up with it, and it doesn't drive me crazy as it did at first." To clarify, just because you work with Gossips doesn't mean your boss is one too. But if gossip is a way of life for most people in your business, it may be time to look for a way out or at least understand that it will be part of your climate.

> **Truth is not exciting enough to those who depend on the characters and lives of their neighbors for all their amusement.**
> George Bancroft

Create Your Own Climate

I have a friend at work, Mike, who rarely gets caught in the gossip trap. On more than one occasion, I have witnessed the same dynamic when Mike enters a room. One day, for instance, I had been making small talk about someone when Mike walked in on the conversation. Quickly the conversation changed course. Something about Mike's presence puts a squelch on gossip. Mike's secret? In spite of atmospheric conditions, Mike creates his own climate. Here is how it works: Once you decide you are not going to be a part of the rumor mill and once you learn to avoid these conversations without inducing guilt in others, people will treat you differently. It is an amazing phenomenon. Once you create your own climate, some people will apologize for speaking ill of others when you are around. Eventually, they will get tired of apologizing and will alter their topics altogether when you approach. I have seen it happen. And when you are not present and your name comes up, someone will say, "You can say what you want about them, but I have never heard them talk bad about people behind their back." That is a wonderful compliment, but the real payoff for creating your own climate comes in being trusted.

> **Gossip is the art of saying nothing in a way that leaves practically nothing unsaid.**
> Walter Winchell

Cut Off Gossips at the Pass

Trafficking in gossip not only hurts the innocent victim— you— but also demeans Gossips and whoever is listening. The good news is that when someone tries to tell you something you'd rather not hear, you don't have to be trapped. There are countless ways to steer clear of unwanted secrets. Simply cut off Gossips at the pass by not listening to their secrets. Use any one of these responses to typical lines from Gossips.

> **Gossips:** *"Can you keep a secret?"*
> You: *"Actually, I can't."*
> **Gossips:** *"There's something I want to tell you, but I'm not sure I should."*
> You: *"Then don't."*
> **Gossips:** *"Wait till I tell you about Mario."*
> You: *"Mind if I wait forever?"*
> **Gossips:** *"Did you hear what people are saying about Barbara?"*
> You: *"You mean that she's so nice that only a jerk would say something bad about her?"*

Your comeback will depend a lot on your style, but you can avoid paving the way for a stream of gossip if you are prepared with some surefire comebacks.

Do You Gain from Gossip?

"It's a total invasion of privacy," snips actress Elizabeth Taylor about the media coverage that inevitably follows each of her many marriages and divorces. The true mark of a professional celebrity is constant complaining about being treated as a celebrity. You may not have a star on Hollywood Boulevard, but you may still enjoy the publicity of being talked about. Do you gain anything from other people's gossip about you?

Find the Good in Gossip

Can gossip ever be good? In a way, it can. In her book *Secrets*, contemporary moralist Sissela Bok provides the best explanation of the good that can come from gossip. She writes, "Cheap, superficial, intrusive, unfounded, even vicious: Surely gossip can be all that. Yet to define it in these ways is to overlook the whole network of human exchanges of information, the need to inquire and learn from the experiences of others, and the importance of not taking everything at face value." We test the parameters of propriety by assessing the reactions of our friends to the shared peccadilloes of others.

There is so much good in the worst of us, and so much bad in the best of us, that it hardly becomes any one of us to talk about the rest of us.

According to John Sabini and Maury Silber, authors of *The Moralities of Everyday Life*, gossiping is our way of exploring how the abstract norms of morality apply to everyday incidents and situations. This is not to say that gossiping is a virtue. It is simply to say that some "gossip" offers a social benefit by substantiating our ethics and simply keeping us updated and informed.

In an eight-week study, Dr. Jack Levine and his research team examined 194 instances of gossip as they occurred in the conversations of 76 male and 120 female students at a large university. Even though the study was limited in scope, the results were surprising. Though 27 percent of the gossip consisted of negative remarks, an equal 27 percent of the remarks were positive or complimentary. The rest of the remarks were mixed.[3]

Leave No Dirt to Dish

For most of her life, television personality Kathie Lee Gifford has followed the same morning ritual. Before breakfast, before her feet even touch the floor, she says a prayer: "Lord, please help me today. Don't let me hurt anyone with my mouth." She writes about it in her autobiography, *I Can't Believe I Said That!* As her many devotees know, Kathie Lee's high-speed chatter does have a way of running on and on. Each morning on *Live with Regis & Kathie Lee*, the effusive cohost pulls up a chair and offers a never-ending supply of chitchat about her husband, Frank Gifford, and their rascally son, Cody. Those daily unfettered chats with cohost Regis Philbin, chats in which she blurts out one-liners on everything in her life, are confidences brought out into the open. Surprisingly, the candor that creates Kathie Lee's appeal is also her insurance against hurtful gossip. Despite her star power, gossip columnists generally leave her alone. She is a celebrity who has beaten the tattlers at their own game. And if you are as bold, you can beat your local Gossips too (without going on national television). Once you open yourself up, you leave little intrigue for the mudslingers. Of course, this strategy is not for everyone, but being an open book just might be your ticket to getting Gossips off your back. Gossips are far more interested in people who are secretive about themselves. Strangely, what you lose in mystery to Gossips you may gain in privacy.

> **Gossip is the lack of a worthy theme.**
> Elbert Hubbard

Know Whom to Tell Your Secrets

The Kathie Lee Gifford method is not for everyone. Some of us have secrets too dark to tell. But if sharing our secrets is so high a risk, why do we do it? We tell secrets to explore what's troubling us and sometimes to get helpful feedback and maybe even to test the reaction to our secret. When other people know our secret, we sometimes feel relief that we are no longer alone. So if you have a secret to share, you really need only one person you can trust, someone who considers it a true privilege to hear what's on your mind. Proverbs 11:13 states this truth: "A gossip betrays a confidence, but a trustworthy man keeps a secret." Sharing a secret with a trustworthy friend can bring the two of you closer together and deepen your relationship. But remember that not every friend is equipped to carry your secrets. I have a friend I care deeply about and always enjoy being with, but I would never trust him with my secrets. He can hardly keep a small secret, and I am not about to trust him with a big one. But does this mean we can't be good friends? Absolutely not. I simply don't relate anything to him I don't want to get around.

If It's Serious and Personal, Act Quickly

In the spring of 1985, a Roman Catholic bishop in Providence, Rhode Island, found himself the subject of unsubstantiated and very damaging gossip. According to the local grapevine, the bishop had been arrested and questioned by the police for sexual misconduct. But it simply wasn't true. So, believing the rumor would eventually die down, the bishop ignored it. Unfortunately, the gossip didn't subside; it gained momentum. "A cruel story runs on wheels," a common saying goes, "and every hand oils the wheels as they run." By not "dignifying the remarks with a response," the bishop allowed the gossip to go unchecked, and his silence implied guilt. However, once the bishop was forced to address the gossip in a local news conference, he dismissed it as having no foundation, and the gossip practically vanished. If you are the victim of serious gossip, you should act quickly. Confront the allegation directly and immediately. To help you do this, you might consider having a credible ally work with you on your behalf.

Find Comfort in God

Working or living with high-maintenance Gossips can be unnerving and sometimes devastating. It can breed deep suspicion and a lack of trust in just about everyone. Gossips cannot "unspeak" their rumor any more than they can snatch back a bullet they have just fired. Once out, the gossip is gone. And the problem is, it won't stop ricocheting until it hurts a number of people. But ultimately, there is One in whom we can find safety, One who is supremely trustworthy. Even though we may not always understand God's ways, we can share our deepest secrets with him in full confidence. In Psalm 62, David wrote, "Find rest, O my soul, in God alone; my hope comes from him. He alone is my rock and my salvation; he is my fortress, I will not be shaken. . . . Trust in him at all times, O people; pour out your hearts to him, for God is our refuge" (Ps. 62:5-6, 8).

CROSS-REFERENCE

For more information related to Gossips, see these other high-maintenance relationships: the Backstabber, the Chameleon, and the Green-Eyed Monster.

7

THE CONTROL FREAK

Unable to Let Go and Let Be

"I AM sure that when we spoke our marriage vows," said Janet, "Bob added 'to have and to hold as long as I'm the boss.'" She was sitting in my office after four years of trying to stand on equal ground with her husband. According to her, Bob never lets go of the reins. Literally. "He would have to be in a complete body cast before he would let me drive the car," she complains. On a few rare occasions that Janet does drive when Bob is in the car, he tells her everything to do: "Stop here." "Speed up." "Pass this guy." "Take our joint checking account, as another example," Janet continues. "Before we met, I was handling my finances just fine. I had an unblemished credit rating." Nonetheless, once Bob entered the picture, he took over handling the money. He writes all the checks and balances the books. "I have no idea most of the time where our finances stand."

"Then there is the remote," Janet said. She was talking about that little gizmo that operates the television. "Need I say more," she gracefully dismissed this easy target. But before the end of our session, Janet summed up her husband this way: "He believes he knows how to do everything, and, by natural right, he is boss of anybody found standing in his vicinity."

Control Freaks come in many guises, from overinvolved spouses to meddling managers. Kelly was an example of the latter. She was a hands-on manager taken to the extreme— oversupervising, hoarding information, refusing to delegate, and resenting independent thought or action. She monitored when her employees arrived in the morning, when they took lunch, and when they left at night, giving overexplicit directions and slapping down people who stepped outside their specific job functions. Needless to say, Kelly's controlling management style did very little to motivate her employees or cultivate innovative thinking. But that didn't bother Kelly. Like most Control Freaks, she was simply looking for compliance.

> **No branch can bear fruit by itself; it must remain in the vine. Neither can you bear fruit unless you remain in me. . . . If you obey my commands, you will remain in my love.**
> **John 15:4, 10**

Some Control Freaks do their dirty work with a smile, while others are verbally abusive. Either way, their relationships suffer. Ever been roped into doing something you didn't want to do? Ever felt as if your preferences were of little consequence? If so, you recognize the frustration that signals you've been had by a high-maintenance Control Freak.

THE ANATOMY OF A CONTROL FREAK

We've all met people like Bob or Kelly. We may know them from work or church. They may be a close associate or a casual acquaintance. They may even be in our own family. One thing is for sure, however; there is no mistaking *who* they are. Control Freaks are the ones in control—or desperately trying to be. Control Freaks have these traits in common: obnoxious, tenacious, invasive, obsessive, perfectionistic, critical, irritable, demanding, and rigid.

Obnoxious

Right off the top, Control Freaks can be characterized as offensive. The term *obnoxious* comes from a Latin word meaning "to harm." And Control Freaks certainly do that. They injure most relationships with their controlling and pernicious ways. The mother of the disciples James and John was a controlling woman. She wanted to make sure that her sons had places of prominence in Christ's kingdom. When the ten disciples learned of her meddling, they were "indignant" (Matt. 20:24). Controllers can be obnoxious.

Tenacious

A little boy was on the back porch playing roughly with his reluctant cat. When they got to making a sizable commotion, his mother heard it and hollered to him, "Johnny, are you pulling the cat's tail?" "No, Mama," the little boy said. "I'm just holding her tail. She's doing all the pulling." Control Freaks are a lot like Johnny. If someone suggests a new way of doing something, for example, they fiercely resist by holding on to the way they want things done, no matter how loud the commotion.

Invasive

I once counseled a man who grew up with a controlling father. Everything he did as a boy was under his father's watchful eye. The father wanted to know more than just where the boy went and who was with him. This father took careful inventory of his son's room. Like a private detective, he would paw through the boy's knapsack and desk drawers on a regular basis, not looking for anything in particular, just being nosy. Control Freaks have little respect for privacy and often snoop in areas that aren't their business.

Obsessive

Control Freaks can become obsessed with pursuing certain issues. For example, Control Freaks may become dogged about a suspicion that something is going wrong in a relationship or that they may get less than a stunning job-performance review. It is the kind of obsession that causes them to lose perspective on everything else.

Perfectionistic

Listen carefully, and you will hear Control Freaks say under their breath, "I can't believe I did that. What a jerk." They will berate themselves for not having everything go exactly right. They demand perfection of themselves and everyone else. Few things are "good enough."

Critical

When people are consumed by the need to control their world, they become critical. Control Freaks can't seem to bite their tongue when they see something go wrong. They blurt out their critique, thinking it will correct the problem. Of course, it rarely does, but this doesn't keep them from trying to control through criticism.

Irritable

When Control Freaks don't get their way, they become irritable. They do not seem to have the ability to go with the flow. When they encounter opposition, no matter how logical, they sulk, become critical, and resort to self-centeredness. Little things will touch off their anger: a messy top on a bottle of mustard, a car that is parked on the "wrong" side of the driveway, a flashlight not put where it is "supposed" to be, and on and on. Anything and everything is fair game for irritable Control Freaks.

Demanding

"Jenny, give me that!" Dan yelled at his wife. When Jenny did not give him her paycheck, Dan yelled again. "Give it to me right now!" Finally Dan grabbed at the paycheck, tearing it as he yanked it from his wife's grasp. Jenny was tired of handing over all financial matters to her controlling husband, but Dan responded in characteristic Control Freak style: by demanding.

Rigid

Control Freaks have one way of doing things—their way. And they can be as inflexible as a drill sergeant in trying to force their methods on you. They want life to run a certain way and aren't willing to budge from their regimen. Their exacting instructions for mowing the lawn, for preparing a salad, for driving a car, and anything else are not to be questioned. They know what's best for everyone and allow others to take the reins only if the others follow their rules.

DO YOU KNOW A CONTROL FREAK?

The following self-test can help you assess whether you are in a high-maintenance relationship with a Control Freak. Identify the person or people who have come to your mind as you have read the preceding paragraphs. Circle the *Y* if the statement is true of the person or people about whom you are thinking. Circle the *N* if the statement does not apply to this person or people.

Y N This person hangs on to projects forever because he or she demands perfection.

Y N Most people would describe this person as picky or critical.

Y N This person loves order and established routines.

Y N This person's controlling behavior alienates others.

Y N Sometimes I suspect this person snoops around in private places.

Y N This person makes me anxious.

Y N Like a bulldog, this person holds on to the way he or she wants things done.

Y N Once this person decides on something, it is settled; all other options cease to exist.

Y N This person can be indecisive because he or she continues to mull over an idea and puts everything else on hold.

Y N If this person doesn't like something, he or she says so.

Y N Most people are surprised by this person's demanding style.

Y N This person has a certain way of doing things and almost never budges.

Y N Hardly anyone would describe this person as flexible and easygoing.

Y N If this person does give in to another's idea, he or she doesn't fully jump on board with it.

Y N If the slightest thing is out of place, this person will find it.

Scoring: Total the number of *Y*s you circled. If you circled ten or more *Y*s, you are certainly in a high-maintenance relationship with a Control Freak.

UNDERSTANDING CONTROL FREAKS

Lillian likes to run the show. When she goes out with friends, for example, she chooses the day, the time, and the restaurant. If that isn't enough, once the restaurant host selects a table, Lillian almost always requests something different. Her friends have come to call it the "Lillian switch." She even tells her companions what to eat, and she dominates the flow of conversation. If Lillian doesn't get her way, she picks apart the place that her friends select or spends the evening sulking.

A few of Lillian's friends put up with her controlling ways, but many leave the relationship. Surely she knows what her dictatorial behavior does to people. So why does she do it? The answer is found at a more unconscious than conscious level. Deep down, Lillian fears being vulnerable. *Control Freaks fear losing control altogether.*

Isn't a little controlling behavior healthy? Sure. Recent research indicates that feeling in control is vital to mental and physical health as well as to happiness at home and satisfaction

Better bend than break. Scottish proverb

at work. In fact, feeling that you are master of your own fate is one of the key traits of happy people, according to my friend David Myers, author of *The Pursuit of Happiness*. What's more, psychologist Judith Rodin has demonstrated in experiments at Yale University how merely feeling in control can alter the functioning of a person's immune system.[1]

Being in control, however, can be too much of a good thing. *Controlling too much creates as much stress as feeling that you have no control at all.* Type A personalities, for example, are often controlling, and they also have a high risk of heart disease.[2] In their pursuit of dominance, Control Freaks often subject themselves to rigid routines that prevent them from enjoying life, to say nothing of the frustration they cause the people around them.

Control Freaks, without knowing it, step over the line from taking charge to being compulsively in control. They can't relax because they always feel at risk of being criticized or shamed for making an utterly human error. And their overly responsible behavior affects other people. Control Freaks simply don't know when and where to stop. Imagine what life would be like if everything we wanted and every goal we hoped to achieve were dictated by the winds of fate or other people's whims. The prospect of such utter powerlessness would be terrifying. *Yet life often feels this terrifying for Control Freaks.*

Sometimes in their attempt to control everything (even the weather), Control Freaks lose control of themselves without warning. It's the story of a golfer who goes berserk after slicing a drive. He hurls the driver down the fairway, takes another club out of the bag, and snaps it in two over his knee. Some Control Freaks literally "freak out."

Control Freaks are driven by feelings of extreme vulnerability and low self-esteem. They are not nearly as self-assured as they appear. Terrified of being criticized, rejected, or exposed in any way, they try to protect themselves by staying in control of every aspect of their lives.

COPING WITH CONTROL FREAKS

Nearly everyone knows Control Freaks. But not everyone knows how to handle them. Whether your Control Freaks are at the office or in the home, you need to know that it is possible to defuse a control attack.

Face the Control Freak Within

In contrast to the Control Freaks in your life, you may feel that you could not even begin to find any controlling tendencies in yourself. But think about it. Aren't you just a little controlling at times? Don't you sometimes become irritable if things aren't done just the way you want them? Don't you ever become a little rigid or demanding? Are you never perfectionistic? Maybe you don't have any of these annoying tendencies. But most of us, if we take an honest look, will discover that we have at least some controlling tendencies from time to time. Of course, this doesn't classify you as a certifiable Control Freak, but it will help you feel a bit of empathy for the Control Freaks in your life.

Don't Take It Personally

Remember that in most cases Control Freaks are trying to protect themselves; they are not trying to hurt you. Don't feel responsible or try to make things better when they get upset. Accusing them of being controlling will only make them more fearful and controlling. Instead, try explaining to them how the behavior makes you feel. You might say something like, "You may not be aware of this, but whenever we get together, it seems that we end up doing things your way. I feel frustrated by that. I'd like to take turns choosing which restaurant or movie we will go to." That is far better— for both you and your controlling friend—than saying, "You never trust me with any decisions." Remember that the behavior of Control Freaks is not a commentary about you; it's a strategy they use to guard themselves from anxiety. So the next time Control Freaks dictate an order, don't take it personally.

Nothing is more terrible than activity without insight.
Thomas Carlyle

Go with the Control

I recently counseled a manager who encountered a Control Freak boss on a new job. The new employee was an eager beaver, very competent. But his boss was sitting on every little thing. The manager's initial impulse was to say to the boss, "Hey, get off my back. That's what I was hired for. Let me be me." The more we explored the likely repercussions of this kind of comment, the more open he became to an alternative.

"Give the boss a chance to see you dot all the *i*'s and cross all the *t*'s and get everything done," I counseled him. The idea behind my strategy was to give the controlling boss some time to lighten up.

The same principle may apply to you. By cooperating with Control Freaks' need to be in control, you can help them calm down and be less controlling. Control Freaks can attempt to control only so much; if they have more confidence in you because you have stayed calm and can work with their input, they may begin to let up on you.

Pinpoint the Need

Defusing Control Freaks depends on finding out what they really want from you. Gerald Piaget, author of *Control Freaks: Who They Are and How to Stop Them from Running Your Life*, asks an important question: "Is the person trying to make you verify that he is right, important, recognized, appreciated, powerful?" To cope, you have to figure out how to give Control Freaks what they want without compromising your own needs. If the Control Freak you know is prompted by anxiety over an important phone call she is waiting to receive, for example, she might snap at you for putting your feet on the coffee table: "Why do you do that? I've told you before how upsetting that is to me."

Rather than accuse her of being irrational and petty, put yourself in her shoes and ask yourself what she is really needing: "I'm sorry, I bet you are eager to get the news from that call you were talking about." A simple statement about what is going on beneath the surface can be soothing to a worried Control Freak. And it will help you weather the controlling storm without getting drenched.

Drown Control Freaks in Information

Think of Control Freaks as overprotective parents. One of the best ways to help them relax is to keep them informed. The more information you give, the less they have to worry and the more they'll let go. This strategy is similar to "going with the control." If you resist your employer's suggestion to hold a meeting with the people in Purchasing because you don't think it's a good use of your time, for example, she'll assume you can't be trusted. The alarm will ring, and your boss may think, *This person is not a team player. This person won't take supervision. This person is trying to hide something.*

> He that complies against his will is of his own opinion still.
> Samuel Butler

Of course you are not trying to hide anything. But she doesn't know that— so tell her. Explain how you received the information you needed over the phone from Purchasing and think it is better to move forward without having a meeting. Better yet, after giving your employer this information, ask if she still thinks the meeting is necessary. You will feel as if you are asking the obvious, but providing Control Freaks with constant information and inviting their input will make your relationship run more smoothly.

Put It in Writing

One of the biggest frustrations I encounter with people who are working for Control Freaks is that their bosses are rarely open to new methods or procedures. Say, for example, you have found a new and improved way for pulling data about past sales activity for year-end reports, but the Control Freaks dismiss the idea out of hand. What can you do? You are convinced that computerizing the office records will save a tremendous amount of time, but the Control Freaks don't buy it. In a situation like this, the best thing to do is put your ideas in writing. Give Control Freaks a chance to think about it. Don't confront them or ask them to discuss it further. Provide lots of reasons why your way will be good. Outflank them with facts. Going through the difficult exercise of gathering data to prove your point may not seem like the best use of your time, but it will be if you end up getting the desired outcome. Hard facts and information are some of the best tools for getting what you need from a controlling employer, spouse, or friend.

Negotiate Your Role

If you are in a relationship with a Control Freak, you probably find yourself debating the same issues over and over: how one drives the car, the way dinner is prepared, and so on. When you identify a boomerang issue like this, call a meeting. Decide together who is best at certain tasks and who should control them. If you are a better cook, you should be in control of the kitchen, and the Control Freak needs to agree to stay clear. If the Control Freak is a better driver, he or she should drive the car when you are together. The trick to making this strategy work is reminding the Control Freak of your agreement. If the person starts telling you how to cut carrots, for example, say, "We agreed that this is my domain, and I am in control here." Maybe such delegated roles seem too formal and prescribed for you. I agree, they can be. But negotiating your preassigned roles can ease your life with a Control Freak and help get him or her to back off.

What's got badly, goes badly.
Irish proverb

Take the Good with the Bad

As difficult as it may be to accept, Control Freaks do offer helpful advice from time to time. Because they give so much advice, however, you may be missing it. Try to pay attention to suggestions and directions that really do help. Look for the positive, not just the negative. In the work setting, for example, Control Freaks are the glue of many organizations. Control Freaks usually take responsibilities seriously and are conscientious, dedicated, ethical, and hardworking. The same is true in a family. So, if you have no patience for Control Freaks, think again next time your airplane is circling to land and you're hoping the air-traffic controller has a boss who demands impeccable attention to detail.

Carve Out Some Autonomy

While finding the good in Control Freaks can be quite helpful, you are guaranteed to find plenty of their "suggestions" unreasonable. That's when it's time for a little assertiveness. Jesus provided a good example of this with Peter. In his own bungling way, Peter was a Control Freak. When Jesus told the disciples he would die and be resurrected, Peter disagreed with him, trying to tell Jesus what he should and shouldn't do. Finally Jesus had to rebuke him sharply: "You are a stumbling block to me; you do not have in mind the things of God, but the things of men" (Matt. 16:23). At times Control Freaks need to face the facts. You can reassure them that you are on their side, while at the same time asserting your own style. **Instead of putting others in their place, try putting yourself in their place.**
I have a friend whose boss was sending her long memos directing her movements. Kathy spoke with her boss privately and said, "You know, I work very well on my own. When I get memos dictating that I do things a certain way, I feel it's counterproductive. I know what a track record you have, and I'm here to support you, but I can produce best with a little autonomy."

Stroke the Controller's Ego

J. Keith Miller, author of *Compelled to Control: Why Relationships Break Down and What Makes Them Well*, believes that chronic Control Freaks will relax and let go only when they begin to feel better about themselves. "When people who have a very low tolerance for painful emotions such as shame and fear feel them surface, urgent internal drives kick in automatically to help them cope." Miller contends that for Controllers to rehabilitate themselves, they must acquire the self-esteem they didn't master in childhood. As a psychologist I know that my job in doing therapy with Control Freaks is in many cases to facilitate a "reparenting" process whereby they can learn to accept that they are valuable and don't need to be ashamed of their needs or their weaknesses. Once this process begins to take hold, once they heighten their sense of self-worth, Control Freaks no longer feel anxious and compelled to dominate. The good news is you don't have to be a psychotherapist to help Control Freaks feel better about themselves. Simply compliment them when you can. Help them feel better about who they are, not what they do.

Know When It's Time to Move On

In some cases, the behavior of Control Freaks is so entrenched that they are afraid to change, and no matter what you do, little works. If you feel that you are up against a brick wall, you run the risk of not only feeling constantly frustrated but also of having your self-esteem and even your job taken from you. In the work setting, for example, Control Freaks can be serious roadblocks to your career. Rachel, a television producer, describes this experience: "He was the only person in the bureau when I was hired by the network headquarters. When I arrived he said, 'All ideas go through me.' He called headquarters every morning, then gave me assignments for the day, on a piecemeal basis. He made sure I had no autonomy. He knew the schedule weeks in advance but didn't tell me until the morning of the shoot. I couldn't work this way."

To err is human, but when the eraser wears out ahead of the pencil, you're overdoing it.
Josh Jenkins

What could this person do? Rachel's colleague was monopolizing information so that everything filtered through him first. He distrusted the other people in the office, discouraged collegial interaction, and didn't want to share credit or plum assignments with his colleagues. The Control Freak ruled. Rachel was faced with the cold fact that she either needed to do the job he required or look for a way out. She decided to leave after fulfilling her one-year contract. She probably made the right decision.

CROSS-REFERENCE

For more information related to Control Freaks, see these other high-maintenance relationships: the Competitor, the Steamroller, and the Wet Blanket.

8

THE BACKSTABBER
Irrepressibly Two-Faced

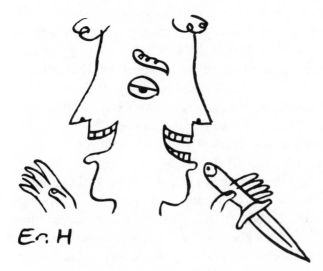

HAVE you ever trusted someone who says one thing to your face and something completely different behind your back?

I have. I worked hard on an important proposal for several months with a supervisor. We were preparing for a meeting in which I would take the lead and present our ideas to an intimidating committee for their approval. My supervisor and I finally came to the place where we both felt ready. We called the meeting and jumped in. Midway through the presentation, it became apparent that our proposal was going nowhere. But if that weren't bad enough, my supervisor left me high and dry. Just minutes before entering the conference room, he was full of enthusiasm and patting me on the back with a have-at-'em attitude. But once we were inside the meeting room, the tables turned, and so did he. No one would have guessed that any of the ideas in the proposal were his. He joined the critiquing and distanced himself from me and the project. "The whole thing, in my opinion, needs an overhaul," I remember him saying in front of the group as I dangled in the wind. I couldn't believe my ears.

I left that meeting stunned and amazed. He left in a hurry.

How could he have changed his position so quickly? How could he have pulled the rug out from under me? How could he stab me in the back when I thought we were on the same team?

The Backstabber is one of the most dangerous and deadly of all the high-maintenance relationships. He sneaks up on you quietly from behind; to your face, the person is probably your biggest fan. But like an undercover assassin, he's out to get you. He holds a knife with your name on it. A figurative knife, that is, aimed straight at your credibility. Properly wielded, it can make mincemeat of your career and anything else that matters.

A patient of mine has worked years to make progress in overcoming a terribly difficult childhood. Only recently has she had the courage to face it fully and talk about it freely. Not long ago, she made a bold step and told a good friend a bit about her background and how she was getting professional help to overcome it. Within a week, her "friend" had used this confidential information to embarrass her in front of others. My blood boiled as she told me about this Backstabber.

Hateful to me as the gates of Hades is that man who hides one thing in his heart and speaks another. Homer

This kind of high-maintenance relationship can occur anywhere — in the workplace, in our homes, and even in church. Backstabbing occurs when a coworker lies low on a project and then grabs credit when it's nearing completion. Backstabbing occurs when a friend agrees with you when the two of you are alone but later sides with your opponents in a social setting. Backstabbing occurs when you share a confidence with someone at church only to learn later that the person has told your story on the prayer chain.

Backstabbing is nothing new. In biblical times, King David experienced the pain of betrayal. He eloquently writes about it in Psalm 55: "If an enemy were insulting me, I could endure it; if a foe were raising himself against me, I could hide from him. But it is you, a man like myself, my companion, my close friend, with whom I once enjoyed sweet fellowship as we walked with the throng at the house of God. . . . My companion attacks his friends; he violates his covenant. His speech is smooth as butter, yet war is in his heart; his words are more soothing than oil, yet they are drawn swords" (Ps. 55:12-14, 20-21).

> **Do not seek revenge or bear a grudge against one of your people, but love your neighbor as yourself.**
> Leviticus 19:18

In the New Testament, we see Christ as a frequent victim of betrayal. Two of Christ's ten closest friends—Peter and Judas—disowned and betrayed him. "After a little while, those standing there went up to Peter and said, 'Surely you are one of them, for your accent gives you away.' Then he began to call down curses on himself and he swore to them, 'I don't know the man!'" (Matt. 26:73-74).

If it were an "enemy" doing the backstabbing, David says, he could endure it. But it is his close friend. Surely Jesus would have understood an enemy lashing out at him, but his own disciples? That's even more painful.

Backstabbing, by the way, is not to be confused with a minor slipup like canceling lunch at the last minute or neglecting to return a phone call. Backstabbing is much more serious. Here's the sign: You know that you have been stabbed when you feel the deep pain of betrayal.

THE ANATOMY OF A BACKSTABBER
The knife Backstabbers use may take the form of bad-mouthing, stealing ideas, undermining meetings, lying, or any other double-crossing tool that suits their fancy. Whatever weapons Backstabbers use, their character traits are fairly consistent. They are usually vindictive, revengeful, deceitful, conniving, resentful, angry, and passive-aggressive.

Vindictive

All of us experience hurts and injustices. But not all of us keep meticulous track of who did them and how we can even the score. Backstabbers do, however. They can tell you who said what about them and why it is wrong at any moment. One of the favorite pastimes of Backstabbers is recounting slights and grievances they've carried for years.

Revengeful

Scripture tells us to turn the other cheek when people hurt us. But Backstabbers just don't buy it. Their motto is: "Don't get mad, get even." An eye for an eye, a tooth for a tooth makes more sense to most Backstabbers. They often are filled with rancor and seething with revenge.

Deceitful

Life would be so much easier if we didn't have to deal with men and women who make promises they have no intention of keeping. Unfortunately, that is one of the marks of Backstabbers.

Conniving

If you are a fan of Shakespeare, you undoubtedly know Iago, the character who missed out on a job he wanted and plotted to get even with the boss, Othello. Iago is like most Backstabbers, concocting plans for someone's downfall. Backstabbers specialize in saying the wrong thing at the wrong time to the wrong person.

Resentful

English poet and humorist Thomas Hood describes the resentful person as a "hedgehog rolled up the wrong way, tormenting himself with his own prickles." This image fits Backstabbers, who often hold on to every offensive word or behavior they have encountered. The problem, of course, is that they eventually unroll to do their damage on others.

Angry

"I am sick and tired of being at the bottom of the totem pole," say most Backstabbers. "I don't have to put up with every jerk who stands in my way, either." Backstabbers ooze anger. They probably won't show it, but they usually are incensed, furious, and mad.

Passive-Aggressive
In all likelihood, Backstabbers are quite pleasant and supportive on the surface. But that's a mask. Behind their smile is a tremendous amount of conflict and resentment. You may therefore find yourself frequently angry at them, not knowing why. Their aggression is expressed passively and is therefore difficult to pinpoint.

DO YOU KNOW A BACKSTABBER?
The following self-test can help you assess whether you are in a high-maintenance relationship with a Backstabber. Identify the person or people who have come to your mind as you have read the preceding paragraphs. Circle the *Y* if the statement is true of the person or people about whom you are thinking. Circle the *N* if the statement does not apply to this person or people.

Y   N   I used to trust this person, and now I don't.

Y   N   This person often says one thing to me and another thing to someone else.

Y   N   Sometimes, when I'm with this person, I think that with friends like this, I don't need enemies.

Y   N   This person agrees with me when we are alone but opposes me when we are in public.

Y   N   I have felt betrayed by this person.

Y   N   This person is looking for a way to get even.

Y   N   I have suffered a great deal of pain from this person's double-dealings.

Y   N   This person is unpredictable and not trustworthy.

Y   N   Being with this person is sometimes like trying to weave in and out of land mines.

Y   N   I'm not the only one who feels betrayed by this person.

Y   N   This person would probably do whatever it takes to reach a goal.

Y   N   This person almost never confronts people to their face; it's always behind their back.

Y   N   This person uses personal information against others.

Y N   Sometimes I feel as if I have been left hanging in the wind by this person.

Y N   I get the feeling this person relishes revenge.

Scoring: Total the number of *Ys* you circled. If you circled ten or more *Ys,* you are certainly in a high-maintenance relationship with a Backstabber.

UNDERSTANDING BACKSTABBERS

A few years ago, Melanie Griffith starred as Tess McGill in the movie *Working Girl,* which is about a thirty-year-old woman who finds out her boss is stealing the credit for her good ideas. In the beginning Tess's boss, Katherine Parker (played by Sigourney Weaver), pretends to be sweet and very interested in becoming a supportive mentor for Tess. Listen to what the new boss says to her assistant during their first important conversation. "I want your input, Tess. I welcome your ideas, and I like to see hard work rewarded. It's a two-way street on my team— and call me Katherine."

For the first time in her career, Tess feels she has found a mentor and an ally. She tells her dating partner how excited she is that finally someone believes in her and respects her. But when Tess gives Katherine an excellent idea for their client to purchase an outstanding radio station, Katherine attempts to steal the credit while assuring Tess the idea has been turned down.

> **False words are not only evil in themselves, but they infect the soul with evil. Socrates**

Rather than being a supportive mentor or friend, Katherine Parker is revealed to be a manipulative adversary. Her sweetness is too saccharine. Her friendliness is an attempt to gain control.

Sometimes it seems Backstabbers' dirty deeds are done simply for selfish purposes. They step on others, side with your adversaries, and steal your ideas to make it to the top. In reality, however, these double-dealings are not always that simple.

The underlying problem with many Backstabbers is a lack of self-esteem. They often feel that they are at a disadvantage, and that's how they justify using devious methods to succeed. They knock you down to pull themselves up. Even if they are your supervisors, Backstabbers operate out of insecurity, believing they have to have perfect order to eliminate any threat to their power. They feel they can do no wrong. If you dare to challenge their authority, be careful. That's when it's time to watch your back.

A sense of powerlessness fuels some Backstabbers. You might hear them complain that nothing they do seems to make any difference. They believe they're getting a raw deal and somebody needs to pay. I know a Backstabber who didn't get a promotion he was counting on, and for the last eight years he has bad-mouthed the man who did. His resentment and frustration, however, has spread, and he backstabs anyone with more responsibility or visibility than he has. This Backstabber, like most, feels weak and thwarts authority at every turn.

> **When a person cannot deceive himself, the chances are against his being able to deceive other people.** Mark Twain

Backstabbers hide buried feelings of inadequacy and injustice. Deep inside, they resent you (for your looks, your intelligence, your hard work), but they won't confess that they are angry or upset or even envious.

COPING WITH BACKSTABBERS

"Loyalty means nothing unless it has at its heart the absolute principle of self-sacrifice," said Woodrow Wilson. I couldn't agree more. That's what makes being the victim of Backstabbers so painful. They put on a front that appears accommodating, loyal, and yes, even sacrificial. Then, without warning, they raise their knife, and by the time you see the glint of the blade, it's almost always too late. But does that mean we are doomed to be victims if we have Backstabbers in our life? No. We can do several things to disarm Backstabbers before they strike. Even if you have already been stabbed, there is hope. Before assessing the aggressor, however, we begin by looking within.

Face the Backstabber Within

Getting even is a natural instinct of our fallen nature. We all know what it feels like to want sweet revenge. We find something seductive about pulling a fast one and swiping some credit or whispering an unkind word. We are tempted to cut an unfair "friend" down to size, but we stop. We know better. We know that revenge is not really that sweet. So we curb it. But knowing that we all have the makings of a Backstabber within us helps us look more graciously at the Backstabbers in our lives.

Watch Your Back

In Dante's *Inferno*, the final circle of hell was reserved for perpetrators of the most heinous sin of all— betrayal. It hurts deeply to learn that someone you trusted has betrayed you. And it's tiresome to be checking your back constantly.[1] I'm not proposing that you should be suspicious of everyone. I am suggesting that you be very careful to share your deepest thoughts only with people whom you know to be trustworthy. Remember that Backstabbers are sneaky, slick, seductive, and sabotaging. They may seem like just the person with whom to share your secrets; that's the way they want it. So if you have reason to believe Backstabbers are running loose around your office or in your circle of friends, be cautious with the things that matter most. Watch your back.

> And while they were eating, he said, "I tell you the truth, one of you will betray me."
> Matthew 26:21

Track Them Down and Smoke Them Out

Most Backstabbers fear being exposed. Once you've detected clear signs of Backstabbers on the warpath, act fast to let them know you know.[2] You may feel tempted to wait and see what happens, but don't. Often the situation can be fixed by calmly chatting with the Backstabbers. If you choose this route, however, walk softly. The goal is to let Backstabbers know that you know what they are doing. When you hear harmful remarks Backstabbers make, ask them what they meant by the remarks. They most likely will try to explain away the comments as a misunderstanding, and that's okay. The point is not to get them to confess or apologize; it is merely to let them know you know. That's all. And a calm question without elaboration lets the Backstabbers know you're aware of what's going on without causing open warfare.

> It is shameful to befriend someone while concealing a grudge.

Stand Up for Fellow Victims

"Ron blows every sales meeting he conducts," a coworker says to you. What's your immediate impulse? If you are like many people, you may want to join in with some of your own negative thoughts about Ron. But if you want to help curb backstabbing in your workplace or anywhere else, resist the temptation. When you see backstabbing happening to someone else, try to stop it. Say firmly to Backstabbers that you just don't believe it. Or point out something good about the person who is being stabbed. After all, someday you may need Ron or somebody else to do the same for you.

Use the Power of the Pen

I spoke with a backstabbing victim who finally decided to confront her tormentor, and it failed miserably. She went into the Backstabber's office to set the score straight. "Instead of making my points," she confessed, "I fell apart. My confidence had been totally undermined." Next, this person spoke with the personnel director of the company about the Backstabber's behavior. "He made me feel even worse. He just told me I wasn't being a team player." Demoralized, this person took a job at another company for less pay. "The experience taught me a lot," she says. "I watch my back now by documenting my work with memos. I'm a whole lot smarter." She learned an important lesson. If you are being stalked by Backstabbers, one of the most important ways you can protect yourself is through writing. By sending a brief memo to a colleague or a superior, you have a paper trail that Backstabbers can't erase.

> Don't place too much confidence in the man who boasts of being as honest as the day is long. Wait until you meet him at night.
> Robert C. Edwards

Build a Network

In the workplace, one of the most important preventative measures you can take to protect yourself against Backstabbers is to make a favorable impression on people around you, supervisors as well as coworkers. Build a network of people who trust you. Have lunch with coworkers and be supportive of your managers. Once these people know you, they will be more likely to come to your defense if snide comments start flying.

Confide in a Confidant

In addition to building a supportive network of friends and coworkers, it's important to have a trustworthy confidant, a person who can act as a mirror, reflecting to you the truth. Ask this person, "Does it seem to you that so-and-so is trying to make me look bad?" A good confidant will shoot straight and let you know if you are just being paranoid or if real danger is on the horizon. Be careful not to use the confidant as a dump site, and be sure your motives are not to disparage the Backstabbers. If you need to talk more about the situation, you may want to do that with another friend who is distant from the relationship.

Let Go of Revenge

If you have been injured by Backstabbers, you may still feel the pain. That's understandable. However, don't let that pain dominate you. When a businessman I know was recently fired, a mutual friend told me with a grim smile, "Well, there is justice in the world. If you wait long enough, things even out!" I asked him what he meant by that comment and found out the man who had been fired had once fired him. When I asked the businessman when the other man had fired him, he told me that dismissal took place fifteen years ago, when they were both young executives! Who needs to think about a grievance like that for fifteen years, or even fifteen months? It's been said that revenge "is a dish best eaten cold"— meaning that the longer you wait, the sweeter it is. I think revenge is a dish best not eaten at all. Storing up pain, nurturing your hurt, plotting revenge— all these punish you more than they do the Backstabbers. So do yourself a favor and let go of revenge. Make the best you can of your life. Enjoy yourself to the full. After all, living well really is the best revenge. Anything else is just sour grapes.

> **Do not take revenge, my friends, but leave room for God's wrath, for it is written: "It is mine to avenge; I will repay," says the Lord.**
> Romans 12:19

CROSS-REFERENCE

For more information related to Backstabbers, see these other high-maintenance relationships: the Gossip, the Cold Shoulder, the Green-Eyed Monster, and the Steamroller.

9
THE COLD SHOULDER
Disengages and Avoids Contact

A GOOD FRIEND of mine recently did an about-face. It used to be that Jerry and I would check in with each other several times a week. We would keep each other informed, talk about work issues, and laugh a lot. On the weekends our families would sometimes share a meal. In many respects I took my relationship with Jerry for granted. It was easygoing, fun, and consistent.

But then something changed. Jerry suddenly seemed distant. He became "busy," and our schedules didn't connect. The relationship I had come to rely on was gone. Intentionally or not, Jerry was giving me the brush-off.

Did I do something wrong? Was it something I said? I was

riddled with questions that presented no easy answers and that left me filled with unresolved tension.

Have you ever had this experience? If so, you know the feeling of betrayal. You know what it's like to have a warm and friendly person suddenly become almost icy cold. You know the Cold Shoulder.

Cold Shoulder relationships come in two forms. As with Jerry, they can appear suddenly. Like a door banging shut against a silent room, Cold Shoulder relationships can surprise us with a quick close. From out of nowhere, it seems, the person decides to treat us differently. And we experience the pain of having our trust torn in two.

Another kind of Cold Shoulder relationship is found in what I call the "steady Cold Shoulders." These are the people who have seemingly *always* been cold and unapproachable. They aren't sending you a message that they are not also sending to nearly everyone else. These people keep the whole world at arm's length.

A respected college administrator, Tim, fell into this category. He was quiet, reserved, and consistently distant—a steady Cold Shoulder. Walking into his office was like walking into a deep freeze. He wasn't mean or grumpy, just disengaged. No warm handshake or words of welcome were necessary for Tim. He offered no signs of personal interest. Even at church he remained expressionless. If you were brave enough to initiate a conversation with him, you ended up carrying the whole thing.

Your reactions to your enemy can hurt you more than your enemy can. Hannah Hurnard

Some people politely dismissed Tim as an introvert, but there was more to Tim than that. After all, he chose a career requiring a great deal of involvement with people. Tim isolated himself from all but a select few people on the college campus. Most of the time Tim used his cold shoulder to control and intimidate. If you couldn't break through his icy exterior, you lived in fear. And that's how he liked it.

Cold Shoulders—whether they are steady or sudden— bring a frosty chill to your system. Unlike Chameleons, who smother you with their eagerness to please, Cold Shoulders leave you longing for a heat wave. Unfortunately, we can often do little to change

Cold Shoulders, but we can do plenty to keep from getting frost-bite from these high-maintenance people.

THE ANATOMY OF A COLD SHOULDER

Ebenezer Scrooge, the Cold Shoulder icon, had a "mentor" in Jacob Marley's ghost. As a result of their relationship, the miserly old man exclaimed, "I will not be the man I was!" And indeed, he changed his ways. Of course this is our hope for all Cold Shoulders, but when we consider the traits that mark their way of relating,

What can't be cured must be endured.
Robert Burton

it would seem a miracle is necessary. Here are some of the primary characteristics of Cold Shoulders: impersonal, indifferent, exclusive, enigmatic, silent, emotionless, unresponsive, and rejecting.

Impersonal

Talking with Cold Shoulders is about as personal as reading a letter addressed to "Occupant." They express little interest in you and your life, and, if anything, they want just the facts. Whether at work or in a social setting, they never ask about your weekend or what is new in your life. If something good has recently happened to you, they don't say a thing about it.

Indifferent

Cold Shoulders can look through you as if they are looking through a window. Little you say seems to matter; they just don't appear to care. They may grunt or simply clear their throats as a response to something you say. If you feel invisible when you are with them, that's because Cold Shoulders are indifferent.

Exclusive

Jennifer suddenly had a new group of friends that were very cliquish. At any gathering, it was understood that no one else was welcome into their social club. "When I tried to sit next to Jennifer in the lunchroom," one of her former friends told me, "I could tell by the nervous look on her face that she wasn't comfortable having me there with her group. I felt as if I were back in high school." Cold Shoulders (especially the steady variety) often have a small clique that no one else dare enter.

Enigmatic

One of the most frustrating traits of Cold Shoulders is that you hardly ever know what they are really thinking. You have a feeling that it is negative because they are withdrawn, but you don't know for sure. For this reason, they often make you feel as if you need to walk on eggshells.

Silent

Like fish underwater, Cold Shoulders can move silently in and out of each passing day. They are often people of few words, especially steady Cold Shoulders. In a committee meeting, for example, they might not speak; they sit, arms folded and motionless, unless someone directly asks them a question.

Emotionless

While sudden Cold Shoulders may still express a wide range of emotions, steady Cold Shoulders are almost always sober faced. They rarely reveal their true emotions. You get the feeling that their tactics have numbed their own feelings.

Unresponsive

With some Cold Shoulders it can be like pulling teeth just to get them to keep you informed about things you absolutely need to know. Cold Shoulders who report to you, for example, might go around you or ignore your requests on matters where you need full cooperation. They may not even return your calls or memos.

Rejecting

"It's as if I have been amputated from her body of friends," is how Merilee described the sudden change in her relationship. "She simply doesn't want anything to do with me. She stamped me 'reject' and tossed me out." Cold Shoulders can be quite rejecting. For a myriad of reasons, they seem to have no problem discarding their connections.

DO YOU KNOW A COLD SHOULDER?

The following self-test can help you assess whether you are in a high-maintenance relationship with a Cold Shoulder. Identify the person or people who have come to your mind as you have read the preceding paragraphs. Circle the Y if the statement is true of the person or people about whom you are thinking. Circle the N if the statement does not apply to this person or people.

Y N   This person shows little personal interest in my life.

Y N   Without warning, this person changed the dynamics of our relationship.

Y N   This person almost seems to push me away.

Y N   I feel that I am consistently getting the brush-off from this person.

Y N   This person keeps most people at arm's length.

Y N   This person's friends form an exclusive group that very few other people can penetrate.

Y N   I am never quite sure what this person is really thinking or feeling.

Y N   I feel rejected by this person.

Y N   This person is unresponsive.

Y N   I cannot trust this person to follow up on things I might request.

Y N   This person's emotions seem one-dimensional.

Y N   This person treats others with a cold shoulder.

Y N   This person gives me the silent treatment.

Y N   I used to feel quite close to this person, but he or she suddenly withdrew from our relationship.

Y N   I feel uncomfortable around this person.

Scoring: Total the number of Ys you circled. If you circled ten or more Ys, you are certainly in a high-maintenance relationship with a Cold Shoulder.

UNDERSTANDING COLD SHOULDERS

In my training as a medical psychologist, I often consulted with physicians who were treating patients suffering from extensive physical burns. Because the healing process takes a long time and because the necessary treatment is so painful, some burn patients simply give up. As the nurses transport them into large tanks where their burned skin is meticulously scrubbed to prevent dangerous infections, these patients will scream, "Don't touch me! Don't touch me!"

Cold Shoulders, in many respects, are like these burn patients. For a number of reasons, they have withdrawn socially and are saying, "Don't touch me!" It is a rather paradoxical maneuver because *Cold Shoulders often push people away at the very times when they most need their comfort and support.*

The Old Testament prophet Jonah may have been a Cold Shoulder, disengaging and avoiding contact even with God. When God called Jonah to preach to the city of Nineveh, the prophet ran away. Only when he was trapped in the belly of the great fish did Jonah stop running and face up to God. Yet when he went to Nineveh and when the people repented from their wickedness, Jonah again withdrew. Sitting outside the city under a vine, Scripture tells us, Jonah whined and pouted.

French novelist Albert Camus said, "The more I accuse myself, the more I have a right to judge you." Cold Shoulders, at least unconsciously, would agree with Camus. *Underlying their rejecting behavior is a sense of self-pity and even shame.* In all likelihood their rejection of you is a reaction to something that has threatened them. They may not even know what it is themselves, but they know that by rejecting you, they can protect themselves.

On the surface, Cold Shoulders may appear content, but that calm exterior is very deceptive. *Underneath the facade of contentment often lie many wounds.* Rather than risk that you may wound them, Cold Shoulders disengage from the relationship.

The same dynamic may be going on in steady Cold Shoulders; except for them, *everyone* is potentially threatening. As a result, steady Cold Shoulders keep everyone at arm's length. Deep down, steady Cold Shoulders don't want to be the way they are, but they can't help themselves because they have never learned how to communicate and express their feelings. And once they master this self-protective style, steady Cold Shoulders find it hard to give up. They learn that by consistently disengaging, they often can manipulate and intimidate others. So the distance serves not only to protect them from personal injury but also to give them power.

> The bitterest enemy and also he who was your friend could again be your friend; love that has grown cold can kindle again.
> Sóren Kierkegaard

Here is the crux of the matter: *Cold Shoulders see vulnerability as weakness.* They may feel the same emotions that other people feel, but if they were to share those feelings, they believe they would lose their power over other people.

COPING WITH COLD SHOULDERS

No one likes to be ignored. No one likes to be left out. Unfortunately, you cannot control other people's climate. If they give you the cold shoulder, you are simply left to adjust. The good news is that you can find ways to respond to this atmospheric condition and make it more comfortable for yourself.

Face the Cold Shoulder Within

Be honest. Have you never given somebody—anybody—the cold shoulder? Most people, at one time or another, have. It seems to be part of the human arsenal of self-protection to withdraw and run for cover when anything threatening looms in a relationship. While you may not have made it a life pattern, you probably know the desire to disengage, to cross to the other side of the street to avoid contact. Tap into this feeling you have experienced (even if you haven't acted on it) to begin the process with a little empathy. Identify the desire to withdraw so that you can get a glimpse into what Cold Shoulders experience.

Many a man claims to have unfailing love, but a faithful man who can find?
Proverbs 20:6

Explore Changes

In most cases, when we encounter Cold Shoulders, we assume that the distance is the other people's initiative. However, we must also be willing to recognize that we may have been the ones to cause the distance. Review the last few months and write down any significant changes in your life (workload, status, health, finances, relationships). As you review the items in the list, ask yourself whether any one of them might have contributed to the rift. Do the same exercise for the Cold Shoulders. You may not know about some of those changes, but do your best. By making these lists, you force yourself to face changes. Don't blow off this exercise by saying "nothing has changed." You might be surprised to discover that from the perspective of the Cold Shoulders, even a little change is quite threatening. If the Cold Shoulder relationship in your life is at your workplace, you can also explore changes in the environment. Is there a recent development that might be creating a subtle rivalry? Are the two of you competing for the same funds or anything else? What about office politics? Are you on different sides of the fence? If you can pinpoint changes in your lives, you will be taking a huge step in unraveling the mystery behind Cold Shoulders' treatment.

Try a Heart-to-Heart Talk

Like many people who encounter Cold Shoulders, Ron had decided not to clear up his difficulties with Kurt, a coworker. Ron resigned himself to see Kurt almost daily at work but not to speak to him unless it was absolutely necessary. As Ron explains, "It's much easier to put up my own wall toward him rather than try to find an opening in the wall he's put up toward me." This seems to make a modicum of sense until you realize that your wall is becoming a self-imposed prison. People almost always pay a high price for relational walls. So before you draw your plans and begin construction—before you say, "Why bring this up with someone who's been ignoring me?"—first build an opportunity to talk face-to-face, one-on-one. Discuss your feelings with the other person and wait for a response. Don't put answers in the person's mouth. Your job is not to vent but to understand by listening. Once you have shared your feelings and the other person has responded, try to explore what brought about the change (if the other person agrees there has been one) and what can remedy the rift. A heart-to-heart talk is sometimes all that is needed to resolve the differences between two people.

> Loneliness and the feeling of being uncared for and unwanted are the greatest poverty.
> Mother Teresa of Calcutta

Count the Cost and Grieve the Loss

My experience with a Cold Shoulder, described at the beginning of this chapter, became a true sore spot for me. To this day I am not exactly sure what brought about the change. I have tried to explore what I could have done, and I have had more than one heart-to-heart with Jerry since then. However, things simply have never been the same. We have an amicable relationship, but it's definitely different. That difference has been hard for me to accept. But at one point I realized that this relationship may never change. If you have come to this point, too, it is time to grieve. Don't make the mistake of keeping your pain alive by holding out hope for something that is doomed for repeated disappointment. Grieve the loss of the relationship, and come to a point of internal resolution. I take comfort in knowing that even Jesus experienced the cold shoulder in his hometown and "could not do any miracles there, except lay his hands on a few sick people and heal them" (Mark 6:5). When he sent his disciples out to the villages, he said: "If any place will not welcome you or listen to you, shake the dust off your feet when you leave" (Mark 6:11). Once I accepted the fact that Jerry and I might never enjoy the camaraderie we once did, I "shook the dust off my feet," and I was able to rest. I was able to breathe deeply, relax, and move on. If someday we once again build our friendship, I will celebrate. But for now, I have put the issue to rest.

> **People are lonely because they build walls, not bridges.**
> Joseph Fort Newton

Don't Mistake the Freeze-Out for Rejection

When it comes to steady Cold Shoulders, it is especially easy to assume that their behavior is a reflection on you. But it isn't always. I have counseled many university students who thought a particular professor was singling them out. "He won't give me the time of day, and I feel like an idiot when I try to be nice to him. Why does he treat me this way?" an especially frustrated student asked. I told her I did not think the professor's behavior was a sign of rejection, and I challenged her to talk to other classmates and see if they ever felt the cold shoulder from the professor. "You were right, Dr. Parrott," she later reported. "Almost everyone I talked to felt the exact same way." Steady Cold Shoulders are not rejecting you. You are not a special case, so don't mistake the big chill for a personal vendetta.

Talk with a Mutual Friend You Respect

When I was in college, I had an experience with a Cold Shoulder. The guy and I weren't best friends, but we were close. When he withdrew, I couldn't figure it out. Finally, one night in the dining hall I asked a mutual friend if he noticed anything different. "Of course—didn't you know that Mike's mom and dad are getting a divorce?" I had no idea. Mike never told me, and I had never even met his parents. How was I to know? That taught me a good lesson about jumping to conclusions and also about the value of checking with a mutual friend. You have to guard against gossip when you talk to a person about someone else, but if you are respectful and use this strategy as a point of clarifying your reality, it can be extremely valuable. So do a little informal research with a colleague or friend. You may find you are not alone, and you may learn something that explains the slight.

Stay out of the Deep Freeze

Some people, not wanting to believe their friend has changed, risk relational frostbite by returning to the Cold Shoulders' deep freeze again and again. In a vain attempt to warm up the Cold Shoulder, they keep trying. The compulsion is understandable: this time it will be different. But it's not. If you find yourself doing this, you don't necessarily have to give up all hope, but you do have to quit putting yourself in a position to get hurt. Lie back. Create enough space for Cold Shoulders to see what they are missing. By backing off, you reverse the roles. There are no guarantees, but I've seen this strategy work, especially in cases in which the Cold Shoulders were feeling smothered by the other person.

> **The cruelest lies are often told in silence.**
> Robert Louis Stevenson

Learn from the Pain

A popular song some years ago said something about not having "time for the pain." Who *does* have time for pain? All of us would rather fly through life, avoiding all tough spots and collisions. But, of course, life doesn't work that way. Most of us grow up with at least some painful experiences that include being left out, ignored, or rejected. As a psychologist, I have met many people who had one or both parents who were emotionally unavailable at crucial times, for example. On the campus where I teach, I have seen plenty of painful moments where someone's romantic attraction suddenly became cold and distant. At all points in our life we have the potential to experience rejection. But whatever the source of the painful memories, these hurts are easily retriggered when people are Cold Shoulders to us. However, through prayerful contemplation, you can use this time to heal raw nerves that have been exposed by the Cold Shoulders. As J. I. Packer has said, "God uses pain and weakness, along with other afflictions, as his chisel for sculpting our lives. Felt weakness deepens dependence on Christ for strength each day. . . . To live with your 'thorn' uncomplainingly is true sanctification."

CROSS-REFERENCE

For more information related to Cold Shoulders, see these other high-maintenance relationships: the Gossip, the Green-Eyed Monster, and the Workhorse.

10

THE GREEN-EYED MONSTER

Seethes with Envy

E.C.H

EVERY person of every age knows what it is like to be jealous of friends, family members, coworkers, or even perfect strangers. Say, for example, your friend shows up at work in an attractive new outfit, and you toss out an honest compliment: "Nice suit. I'm jealous." You'd like a new outfit too. Who wouldn't? And unless there is something more to your message, you have little to worry about. But if you're secretly hoping your coworker's clothes get stained over lunch, look out! That's when gentle jealousy turns into evil envy.

Envy is not a gentle emotion. It's aggressive. Unlike jealousy, which focuses on possessing what you desire, envy focuses on taking something you desire away from the person who owns it. Envy is not just wanting what the other person has; envy is wanting the other person *not* to have it. In everyday conversation, of course, the two terms are often used interchangeably. But they are quite different.

Why do we say a person turns green with envy? Well, perhaps it's the most sickening of the sins—very different from the six other deadly sins. Envy, unlike gluttony, lust, pride, and the others, isn't even pleasurable. It is gratuitous, done for its own sake. Yet by any standard, envy is a tortuous, tormenting, even murderous emotion. Cain slew Abel, remember, because Abel's sacrifice was more pleasing to the Lord. The Bible is filled with stories of envy: Jacob and Esau, Leah and Rachel, Joseph and his brothers, even Herod and Jesus. Envy feeds on itself and rots the bones. Poet John Milton was right in making it the devil's own emotion. In Milton's *Paradise Lost*, Satan, seeing Adam and Eve in love in Paradise, envies them and plots their fall. Envy has no positive goal whatsoever.

> **Envy: the green sickness.**
> William Shakespeare

No matter who is envied and who does the envying, the emotion is destructive. It dehumanizes both people. Consider the enduring fairy tale about Cinderella. She is the envy of her cruel stepmother and ugly stepsisters, and their terrible malice toward her has sentenced her to servitude and suffering.

Indeed, to be the object of envy can be as painful as feeling envious of someone else. Surprisingly few people have written about how to handle envy when you are the object of it. To be envied is to have something venomous aimed at you. And little attention has been given to finding the right antivenin. For too long, people at home and in the workplace have been haunted by the Green-Eyed Monster and have not known what to do.

THE ANATOMY OF A GREEN-EYED MONSTER

You may be the target of envy in a romantic relationship, at work, at school, with friends, or in your family. The Green-Eyed Monster can appear almost anywhere. But when it does, it usually expresses itself with these common traits: hurtful, angry, competitive, anguished, greedy, faultfinding, and self-pitying.

Hurtful

Remember when Iraqi president Saddam Hussein torched Kuwaiti oil fields he could not harvest and polluted beaches he had to abandon? That was envy in Technicolor. Causing pain is a symptom of chronic envy. If Green-Eyed Monsters cannot have heaven, they will do their best to raise hell in the lives of others by hurting whatever they care about.

Angry

Envy always travels with its cousin anger. I know a man who, when he saw his former female dating partner with another man, became so enraged that he walked up to the couple and started to swing at the other man. Anger is the part of envy that enables the Monster to keep the envied person at arm's length, thereby allowing him or her to try and restore a little self-esteem.

Competitive

Anytime you believe you have to be the best in everything, whether it be decorating, cooking, writing, making friends, giving speeches, or anything else, you open yourself up to envy. Needless to say, Green-Eyed Monsters do just that. They draw their self-worth from what they have and how they do. And when what they have is not better than what everyone else has— which it never is— envy takes over. Envy puts Monsters on a never-ending race they can never, ever win.

As rust corrupts iron, so envy corrupts man.
Antisthenes

Anguished

Envy can take a variety of forms, from an abrupt burst of resentment to a slow-burning bitterness. However it comes about, envy is marked by a deep sense of grief, pain, sorrow, and suffering. When people set their sights on others and measure their success against that yardstick, they are doomed to anguish.

Greedy

"The covetous man is ever in want," said Horace Bushnell. Rarely, if ever, are Green-Eyed Monsters contented. They are green with greed. Like investors watching their stock go down or like a losing team watching the clock running down, they are desperate for more time, money, looks, intelligence, friends, opportunities, you name it.

Faultfinding

Since Green-Eyed Monsters are always comparing themselves to others, their self-esteem suffers. One way they try to bolster their own sense of well-being is to find fault with others. Soon faultfinding becomes a way of life. If they can undermine your success, they think they will feel better about themselves. "She married him for his money. How else do you think he could find a wife?" The Monsters are born iconoclasts, who thrive on exposing other people's defects. Indeed, their greatest pleasures are in the bringing down of those who are on the rise.

Self-Pitying

Whine, whine, whine. Envy feeds on whiny self-pity: "Why can't I get a break now and then?" "Nobody pays attention to what I do." "Everybody has it better than I do." Writer and preacher Charles Swindoll once said about self-pity, "Cuddle and nurse it as an infant, and you'll have on your hands in a brief period of time a beast, a monster, a raging, coarse brute that will spread the poison of bitterness and paranoia throughout your system."

DO YOU KNOW A GREEN-EYED MONSTER?

The following self-test can help you assess whether you are in a high-maintenance relationship with a Green-Eyed Monster. Identify the person or people who have come to your mind as you have read the preceding paragraphs. Circle the *Y* if the statement is true of the person or people about whom you are thinking. Circle the *N* if the statement does not apply to this person or people.

Y   N   This person constantly compares himself or herself to other people.

Y   N   This person belittles the accomplishments, talents, or appearance of others.

Y   N   This person seems pleased when other people suffer setbacks.

Y N This person has an uncanny knack for finding fault with others.

Y N The success of another can set this person into a tailspin of self-pity.

Y N If this person can't enjoy something, he or she will do whatever possible to see that others don't enjoy it either.

Y N This person has a need to pull down successful people.

Y N This person treats life like a competition, always jockeying for the best position.

Y N At times this person can become consumed with rage at someone else's success.

Y N This person is an expert at undermining other people's progress and success.

Y N "Enough" is never enough for this person.

Y N This person always wants more of what other people have.

Y N This person hoards information that can be used to make him or her look better.

Y N This person suffers when others succeed.

Y N Even when this person is blatantly jealous, he or she will deny it.

Scoring: Total the number of Ys you circled. If you circled ten or more Ys, you are certainly in a high-maintenance relationship with a Green-Eyed Monster.

UNDERSTANDING GREEN-EYED MONSTERS

The devil was crossing the desert and came upon a few of his fiends who were tempting a holy man who easily shook off their evil suggestions. The devil watched their failure and then stepped in to give them a lesson: "Permit me to show you how it is done." With that he whispered to the holy man, "Your brother was just made bishop of Alexandria." An incredible scowl of jealousy clouded the serene face of the man, and his whole demeanor drooped. "That," said the devil to his imps, "is what I recommend."

Hearing something good about a rival (even a relative) can deplete anyone of goodwill. From nowhere jealousy and envy can strike like a missile. But why would anyone become consumed by envy? Consider these facts:

- Not everyone who expects to own a home or reach other financial aims will realize these goals.
- Not everyone who expects to attend undergraduate or graduate school will be able to afford it.
- Not everyone who expects to reach career objectives will succeed.
- Not everyone who expects to marry will find a spouse.
- Not everyone who expects to be a parent will be able to have a family.

This short list of people's hopes and expectations could go on for several pages. The point is that we can't always get what we want. As disappointment grows, and as ambitions and desires are thwarted, conditions become ripe for the toxic fumes of envy.

In many cases, the seeds of envy can be found in early childhood. Green-Eyed Monsters were most likely reared on high expectations and were not trained to cope with limitations. They grew up as kids who had everything, and they don't feel they should have to do without. If they see something they want, they feel they should have it. And if you stand between them and what they desire, their sense of entitlement drives them to the ugly emotion of envy. It's that simple.

A person is truly great when he is not envious of his rival's success.

Green-Eyed Monsters rear their heads because they feel deprived. The opening lines of Joyce Carol Oates's "House Hunting," her award-winning short story about a young couple who has lost a baby, describes such a precipitating event: "How subtly the season of mourning shaded into a season of envy. To their knowledge they had never been envious people, but suddenly they caught themselves staring at families, young parents with their children . . . strangers whose happiness grated with the irritation of steel wool against the skin." The feelings of deprivation this couple experienced occurred in relation to their assessment of their neighbors' condition. The couple wanted what other people around them had, a privilege to which they felt they were entitled.

People often envy what is close to them, not what is distant. Historically, Aristotle was the first to devote real thought to the problem, calling envy "the sin against the brother," asserting that envy is felt most keenly by two people of the same age and similar interests. Green-Eyed Monsters who have their sights on earning lots of money will probably envy their neighbors or friends who earn more money long before they will envy the Rockefellers. The newly graduated electrical engineer who is looking for work will envy a classmate's new job but have little problem with an actor friend who gets a plum role in a play. The closer a situation comes to matching the Green-Eyed Monster's own identity, the higher the stakes become and the more likely envy is to erupt.

> **A heart at peace gives life to the body, but envy rots the bones.**
> Proverbs 14:30

The strange thing is that most Green-Eyed Monsters don't want to feel envious. That's an important point in understanding their behavior. Green-Eyed Monsters would often rather be big-spirited and generous, but they find they just can't feel that way.

At the center of the psychological struggle for Green-Eyed Monsters is an empty sense that life is passing them by. They often feel a deep disappointment in themselves. They feel that they are not living out their potential. Joseph Epstein, a literary scholar and author of *Ambition: The Secret Passion,* calls it "disinterested envy" and suggests that what causes this feeling is "one's own unmistakable sense that one ought to get more out of oneself." High-

> **Envy is like a disease; it consumes the soul.**
> Jewish proverb

maintenance envymongers hear about a classmate who is cleaning up in real estate or about a business friend, five years their junior, who has been named president of a large corporation, and they feel a pang of near hatred— not just because they want what these others have and not because they don't want them to have it, but because the other people's success reminds them that they are not living their own life to the fullest. They feel diminished by other people's successes. That's what makes them green with envy.

COPING WITH GREEN-EYED MONSTERS

Green-Eyed Monsters can poison a valued friendship, make family gatherings acrimonious, or turn the workplace into a torture chamber. And it's a catch-22. If you do well, if you succeed, it seems, they will resent you. But if you try to be kind to the people who envy you, they may think you are condescending. Even a whiff of pity in your attitude can be natural gas to the fires of envy. So what is left for the envied? Thankfully, you have plenty of options. Here are some of the most effective ways of managing this high-maintenance Monster.

Recognize the Green-Eyed Monster Within

It's easy to deny our envious ways. After all, we cloak them in other emotions. For example, a friend of yours seems to have a more attentive spouse than yours, a child who is more recognized than your child, or more opportunities to travel than you do. Self-pity creeps in, and unconsciously you feel inferior. Envy results. But being envious never gained anyone sympathy, so you begin to see the situation as unfair and unjust. In this way, envy becomes righteous resentment, which in turn gives you the "right" to protest. Sound familiar? If not, you are either extremely rare or still in denial.

> **Too many Christians envy the sinners their pleasure and the saints their joy because they don't have either one.**
> Martin Luther

Everyone carries a little envy. It's part of being human. In fact, a cross-cultural study of relationship jealousy and envy conducted by psychologists Martin Daly and Margo Wilson of McMaster University found these emotions present in every culture they investigated. Moreover, they found that every person in a significant relationship experiences them from time to time. To a certain degree, every mature human being can identify with the feelings of chronic envy by comparing them to our own milder forms of competitive insecurity. Granted, you may more quickly recognize these emotions as counterproductive, but owning up to this part of yourself, no matter how small, will help you empathize with the Green-Eyed Monsters in your life.

Shower the People Who Envy You with Prayer

"You have heard that it was said, 'Love your neighbor and hate your enemy.' But I tell you: Love your enemies and pray for those who persecute you" (Matt. 5:43-44). With this straightforward injunction found in the Sermon on the Mount, Jesus proclaimed a strategy for revolutionizing the human heart. How preposterous it must have sounded the first time he preached it —praying for those who persecute you? But this action is the single most important way of handling people who envy you. Without loving those who envy us, living or working with envious people becomes a game of keeping score; taking an eye for an eye. But "turning the other cheek" and "going the extra mile" free the envied from the tyranny of Green-Eyed Monsters. These actions protect us from lashing out and free us from needless worry. So as much as it is possible, learn to include Green-Eyed Monsters in your prayers, and thank God for them—even if you have to grit your teeth to do it at first.

> **Envy slays itself by its own arrows.**
> Greek proverb

Don't Take Envy Attacks Personally

One of the reasons we get stung by the evil of envy is that we take its attacks personally. What we fail to realize is that Green-Eyed Monsters don't see us as we really are. They turn their objects of envy into an idealized role. "Envy always makes you into a thing," says Ann Ulanov, author of *Cinderella and Her Sisters*. "If you're the envied one, you're either seen as an idealized perfect object or as the root of all the other person's suffering. You're not seen as yourself. You're just looked at for the part of you that the other person wants to steal or take." Realizing that Green-Eyed Monsters see you as a "thing" can help you disengage a bit from any attacks and not take them personally. Remember that how you see yourself is far more important than how Green-Eyed Monsters see you.

Find a Safe Community

If you are the envy of a Green-Eyed Monster, you may feel yourself isolated from the community. Humorist Garrison Keillor chides a resident of his mythical Lake Wobegon: "Who do you think you are? You're not so smart. You're from Lake Wobegon. You shouldn't think you're somebody. You're no better than the rest of us." This painful phenomenon happens in real towns too. And if you have experienced being shut out of a community because people envy you, find a place where people accept you as you are. This is crucial to maintaining accountability and a healthy sense of social balance. You need to find a place where your gifts are appreciated and where you can let down your guard. You need a place where you can be vulnerable. Dr. Scott Peck, in *The Different Drum*, says, "There can be no community without vulnerability." He is right.

Don't Hide Your Hard Work

I have a friend who wrote a book but decided not to tell anyone she was doing it because she didn't want people to think she was brash. She chose not to tell other people about the book until the first draft was complete or until she had a contract with a publisher. All the while she was quietly doing research, painstakingly filing notes, crafting a careful outline, and doing the hard work of writing drafts. For more than two years she wrote, telling only a few of her very closest friends. Even after she signed a contract with a publisher, she kept quiet. That was probably a mistake. When the book was released, she excitedly gave a copy to each of her colleagues. She was surprised by the cold reception her colleagues gave the book. Nobody said a thing to her about her book. Three weeks later, while standing at the copy machine, she overheard a conversation that was most likely meant to be overheard: "I doubt she even did it herself. We would have known if she had been working that hard on something outside of the office." That same day, an older coworker came into my friend's office and blurted out: "I can't believe you didn't tell us about this book! I had no idea you were working on it. How am I supposed to feel?" My friend was shocked, devastated, crushed. She could have alleviated at least some of their envy by letting them see the hard work that went into accomplishing her goal.

> The Lord looked with favor on Abel and his offering, but on Cain and his offering he did not look with favor. So Cain was very angry, and his face was downcast.
> Genesis 4:4-5

Catch Green-Eyed Monsters Succeeding

Envious people are often in denial. It is their way of avoiding the pain of acknowledging that their dissatisfaction is caused not by you but by their own feelings of failure. For this reason, give them grace and be liberal with your compliments. Look for areas where Green-Eyed Monsters are succeeding, and praise them for their efforts. If you hear that they have accomplished something worthwhile, pick up the phone and celebrate their success. Before you get carried away with this good deed, however, ask yourself why you are doing it. If you are not sincere in your praise, Green-Eyed Monsters will sense it, and their envy will only be exacerbated.

Accept a Little Envy as the Price You Pay for Success

Face the facts—anyone and everyone can be the target of envy. Trying to defend against it completely can be futile. And don't think you can avoid it if you just stay low and move fast. If you try to respond by withdrawing, you will be renounced as cold and aloof. And if you try to appease the envious people with rational explanations, they won't always listen to you. Just as Cinderella's sisters scorned her attempts to reach them, an envied person "learns that any efforts to be nice will only intensify the break," according to Ann Ulanov. "The envied person has run into a wall with no opening and no way around it." It sounds cruel, but it's reality. With some people in certain times you will be enveloped by their envy and have nowhere to turn. Accept a little envy as the price you pay for who you are and what you do.

> **For where you have envy and selfish ambition, there you find disorder and every evil practice.**
> **James 3:16**

Take Special Care If You Are a "Young Buck"

One situation is so ripe for envy that it requires special attention. It occurs whenever a "young buck" is crowding in on the old guard. Remember what happened between Saul and David after David's earliest military campaigns. For years Saul had been Israel's undisputed war hero. But then David, who had the touch of God on him, gained the people's attention with his victories in battle. And Saul, the old warrior, felt the demons beginning to stir in him. How ominous it was for Saul to see David win the acclaim he had come to enjoy as king. How threatening to hear the crowds roaring for David and women sing about him: "Saul has slain his thousands and David his tens of thousands" (1 Sam. 18:7). In this classic case of a star eclipsed by a superstar, Saul sees, fears, and murderously resents the changing of the guard.

Your superiors may too. If you are a young buck on a fast track, take special care not to wave your flag too high or play your horn too loudly. Honor those who have gone before you. For as English dramatist Francis Beaumont put it, "Envy, like the worm, never runs but to the fairest fruit; like a cunning bloodhound, it singles out the fattest deer in the flock."

Beware of Being Had

Tina worked extremely hard to achieve success as a real estate agent. Her satisfaction turned sour, however, when her company hired a new agent who managed to work less yet made more sales. Tina hid her dislike of the new agent by offering to take her phone messages while she was out. When Tina began making more sales than her rival, no one made the connection between this turn of events and Tina's tendency to "forget" to deliver certain phone messages. I hope that the Green-Eyed Monsters in your life don't behave as Tina did. But beware of people who envy you.

CROSS-REFERENCE

For more information related to Green-Eyed Monsters, see these other high-maintenance relationships: the Competitor, the Backstabber, and the Gossip.

11

THE VOLCANO

Builds Steam and
Is Ready to Erupt

GROWING up, most of us don't get much practice with healthy anger. In fact, we're taught to fear such feelings. The truth is that anger is normal and natural. We are not responsible for being angry, only for how we respond to and use anger once it appears. The apostle Paul understood this when he said, "In your anger do not sin" (Eph. 4:26).

Plainly put, humans were created with a capacity to experience passionate anger. There is no doubting that. But for some quick-tempered people, anger becomes more than a human emotion. It becomes a chronic pattern of self-defeating rage whose trigger is unpredictable. Such is the case of Volcanoes, people who are constantly building steam and are all too ready to erupt. Hostility is the hallmark of their personality.

My friends David Stoop and Stephen Arterburn tell the story of Cliff, whose volcanic responses may seem improbable— until you meet a Volcano. Frustrated with a lawn mower that wouldn't start, Cliff walked into his house, through the kitchen, past his wife. "Is the mower broken?" she asked Cliff. He didn't respond. He didn't even acknowledge her presence. He went to his den, grabbed his prized deer rifle, and headed back out to his yard.

His wife, now watching from her kitchen window, hollered to her husband, "What are you doing?" Again he said nothing and walked toward the mower. About ten feet from the machine, he stopped, slid several shells into the rifle's magazine, and bolted a shell into the chamber. Cliff lifted the rifle, took aim at the mower, and fired.

> **A quick-tempered man does foolish things.**
> Proverbs 14:17

Sparks and tiny shreds of metal exploded from the defenseless lawn mower. It was a wonder Cliff wasn't struck by shrapnel.[1]

It sounds preposterous. But such stories are not surprising to anyone who has encountered Volcanoes. In their adult tantrums they throw chairs, smash dishes, dent cars, all in a vain attempt to appease their ever-rumbling temper. Anything can become a target of their wrath, from lawn mowers to loved ones. Whether personal or political, petty or weighty, every issue is fair game to Volcanoes who feel thwarted or threatened.

Volcanoes speak fluent punctuation: "?*!!#." They snarl and growl; they hiss and smolder. Volcanoes sometimes lie dormant, quietly building steam, but in a moment's notice, they can erupt in violent fury, spewing red-hot ash and cinders on anyone who happens to be nearby.

If you have ever experienced one of these eruptions, or worse, are stuck in the lava from Volcanoes, take heart. This chapter contains some of the most effective strategies known for keeping hostile Volcanoes from getting out of control.

THE ANATOMY OF A VOLCANO

Occasionally my wife, Leslie, and I speak for Youth with a Mission at their headquarters in Kona, Hawaii. As a result, we have learned a lot about the volcanoes and lava formations that dominate the island. Seeing these geological volcanoes has helped me understand a few characteristics of human Volcanoes: unstable, cynical, faultfinding, conspiratorial, rude, revengeful, selfish, and prone to guilt.

Unstable

Have you ever sat in a chair that had one wobbly leg? It may have been strong enough to hold you up, but you weren't too sure how much you could trust it. That's the way it is with a lot of Volcanoes. Their unstable demeanor makes it difficult, if not impossible, to rely too heavily on them. Emotionally, you are just never sure how Volcanoes will behave.

Cynical

Volcanoes are not the most optimistic people you will ever meet. They tend to question people's motives and expect the worst from others. Cynicism seems to course through their veins and add to their trigger-happy anger. As Ralph Waldo Emerson put it, "A cynic can chill and dishearten with a single word."

Faultfinding

God help the person who has done something that does not meet the expectations of Volcanoes. If things are not perfect, they feel completely justified in pulling out the stops and letting loose every ounce of pent-up frustration. Volcanoes have a keen eye for seeing mistakes—real and imagined.

Conspiratorial

Volcanoes are often looking over their shoulder to see who might be listening. They believe that no one can be trusted; thus, everyone is a potential threat. It is only natural, then, that Volcanoes often feel that "everyone" is out to get them, to do them harm.

Rude

How else can you say it? Volcanoes are just plain rude. They blow their stack at a grocery-store clerk who is trying to be helpful but can't find a certain item. Never mind that the clerk is trying.

Volcanoes make snide remarks and fume out of the store. Volcanoes throw courtesy and patience out the window.

Revengeful

You know the phrase. You've seen it on buttons and bumper stickers. "I don't get mad, I get even." For Volcanoes, however, this is no joke. They are driven to retaliation and revenge. They want to settle the score. It becomes their driving obsession whenever they feel they have been mistreated. They plan countless ways of vindicating themselves, all the while neglecting the ancient wisdom that says, "He who seeks revenge digs two graves."

Selfish

Empathy is a quality that is glaringly absent from the repertoire of Volcanoes. They seem incapable of understanding another person's perspective and do little to put themselves in another's shoes. For the most part, Volcanoes focus on their own needs, great and small, and they can erupt with a vengeance if you are not just as concerned about getting their needs met as they are.

Prone to Guilt

One of the bugs in the mental computer of Volcanoes is a tendency toward making internal "should" statements. They tell themselves that things should be the way they hoped or expected them to be. And when they are not, they resort to anger. Volcanoes may even try to motivate themselves with *shoulds,* as if a little guilt would help them perform better.

DO YOU KNOW A VOLCANO?

The following self-test can help you assess whether you are in a high-maintenance relationship with a Volcano. Identify the person or people who have come to your mind as you have read the preceding paragraphs. Circle the *Y* if the statement is true of the person or people about whom you are thinking. Circle the *N* if the statement does not apply to this person or people.

Y   N   At an emotional level, this person is unstable.

Y   N   This person likes to get back at others.

Y N   People who know this person well would say that he or she is cynical.

Y N   This person has an eagle eye for other people's faults.

Y N   It sometimes doesn't take much to put this person over the edge.

Y N   Being with this person is sometimes like being with a time bomb that may explode.

Y N   Plainly said, this person can be rude.

Y N   This person often feels as if others are out to get him or her.

Y N   This person has a low level of empathy for others.

Y N   This person has a short fuse.

Y N   When things don't go this person's way, he or she resorts to anger.

Y N   This person is often focused on "evening the score."

Y N   Shocking things sometimes happen when this person gets angry.

Y N   This person can sometimes lose his or her temper in public.

Y N   It's difficult to predict what will upset this person.

Scoring: Total the number of Ys you circled. If you circled ten or more Ys, you are certainly in a high-maintenance relationship with a Volcano.

UNDERSTANDING VOLCANOES

Why is it that while most people let minor aggravations slide, Volcanoes can't contain their rage? Why are they so easily provoked? Researchers provide several answers. In experiments using deliberate provocations such as frustrating math problems and rude assistants, *scientists have identified a potentially catastrophic chain reaction in Volcanoes.* As a result of the provocation, the brain signals the adrenal glands to dump an extra dose of stress hormones, including adrenaline, into the bloodstream; spurred on by adrenaline, the heart races, and blood pressure rises. Once this takes place, the strain of hormone-laden blood raging unchecked through the arteries causes people's blood to "boil," and they erupt in anger.

But these angry outbursts cannot be explained by biology alone.

Research psychologists point out that *some Volcanoes use anger as a defense against potentially painful relationships.* They often have grown up in homes where they were put down, rejected, unjustly criticized, or even abused. Their learned response to this negative environment is to protect themselves with a heavy armor of anger and aggression. They have been burned. They have learned that relationships are painful, and they are not about to let others take advantage of them. Anger, then, becomes a way of life. It is a kind of insulation from potential psychic pain.

The apostle Paul may have used anger in this way when he erupted at Mark for leaving him as a young missionary. The incident caused a deep rift between Paul and Barnabas. "They had a such a sharp disagreement that they parted company" (Acts 15:39). Paul was not about to be burned again. As Scripture says, "Paul did not think it wise to take Mark, because he had deserted them in Pamphylia and had not continued with them in the work" (Acts 15:38). However, even though Paul was angry, he was not a Volcano. In fact, other New Testament letters suggest that Paul set this issue right: "My fellow prisoner Aristarchus sends you his greetings, as does Mark, the cousin of Barnabas. (You have received instructions about him; if he comes to you, welcome him.) . . . These are the only Jews among my fellow workers for the kingdom of God, and they have proved a comfort to me" (Col. 4:10-11).

If men would consider not so much where they differ, as wherein they agree, there would be far less of uncharitableness and angry feeling in the world. Joseph Addison

Another factor shaping the behavior of Volcanoes is the modeling provided by one or both parents. A comprehensive longitudinal study of grade-school children in New York revealed that parents' aggressive behavior at home is closely associated with aggressiveness in children at school.[2] We hardly need a study, however, to tell us that children model their parents. If children grow up in homes where dads fly off the handle and control their families with physical and verbal abuse, it makes sense to conclude that the children will learn to use anger in the same way. These kids are simply Volcanoes in the making.

Perhaps the most clearly defined causal factor of chronic eruptions of

anger is found in the Volcano's cynical mistrust of others. Expecting that others will mistreat them, Volcanoes are on the lookout for bad behavior— and usually find it. This mistrust generates frequent anger, and that anger, combined with a lack of empathy for others, leads Volcanoes to express their hostility overtly. For example, if a Volcano is waiting for an elevator and the elevator stops two floors above for a bit longer than normal, the Volcano begins to think, "How inconsiderate! You'd think if people wanted to carry on a conversation, they'd get off the elevator so I could get to where I'm going!" The

> **An angry man opens his mouth and shuts up his eyes. Cato**

Volcano cannot see or hear the people two floors above and has no way of knowing what is really holding up the elevator. Yet, in the span of a few seconds, the Volcano's cynical mistrust has led him or her to draw hostile conclusions about the unseen people in the elevator, their selfish motives, and their inconsiderate behavior. That's the way of high-maintenance Volcanoes.

COPING WITH VOLCANOES

When Mount Saint Helens erupted in Washington several years ago, everyone in the Pacific Northwest was affected to some degree or another by the aftermath. I can remember sweeping volcano ash from the steps of a friend's house in Portland, Oregon, hundreds of miles away. And just as geological eruptions like this force people to cope in ways they never expected, so do the eruptions of human Volcanoes. Thankfully, however, we have plenty of proven techniques for coping with angry outbursts—even when we have little warning.

Accept the Volcano Within

In his book *Emotions: Can You Trust Them?* Dr. James Dobson states that four primary situations will elicit anger in just about anyone. The first is fatigue. When people are tired, run-down, and hungry, they are more susceptible to anger. Second is embarrassment. When we are belittled or demoralized in a public setting, anger is often the result. Third is frustration. A thwarted plan of almost any magnitude can set many people off. Finally, there is rejection. Often when a person is hurt, anger rears its head. The point is that anger is an emotion we all experience. When we encounter Volcanoes and become repulsed by their angry eruptions, we naturally want to run in the opposite direction. We say, "What's their problem? I would never behave like that!" The truth is that at some point most of us erupt irrationally. And while we may not make it a lifestyle as the Volcano does, we still get irrepressibly angry at times. So own up to this emotion and do what you can to empathize with Volcanoes. It will help ease the pressure in your relationship.

Don't Bury Your Own Anger

On a recent trip to London I visited the "war rooms" where Winston Churchill worked safely underground during World War II. While there, I learned that the bombs dropped during this war are still killing people in Europe. They turn up — and sometimes blow up—at construction sites, in fishing nets, or on beaches fifty years after the guns have fallen silent. Thirteen old bombs exploded in France last year alone. Undetected bombs become more dangerous with time because corrosion can expose the detonator. What is true of bombs that are not dealt with is also true of unresolved anger. Buried anger explodes when we least expect it. That's the pitfall of trying to cope with the anger of Volcanoes by trying to diminish and downplay our own. It's a natural tactic. After all, when we are faced with the war-at-all-costs mentality of Volcanoes, we want peace at any price. This misguided thinking reasons, "If I never express my anger, they will certainly tone down theirs."

Anybody can become angry—that is easy; but to be angry with the right person, and to the right degree, and at the right time, and for the right purpose, and in the right way—that is not within everybody's power and is not easy.
Aristotle

In my work as a psychologist, I have seen many spouses who say, "No, of course I'm not angry!" when they really are seething with rage. Most are convinced that people would not like them if they aired their ire, that yelling at someone was pretty much the same as murder, and that once they started, they'd never recompose themselves. But burying our anger is a dangerous practice. Not only does it make it next to impossible to keep our stomach lining intact, but it makes it difficult to build genuine relationships. If we are unable to risk rage now and then, we sacrifice intimacy and create a minefield of angry outbursts ready to erupt without reason.

Don't Be a Scapegoat

"Watch out, Mom, kids, cats, and dogs! Here comes Dad, and he's upset again!" is a common attitude in homes where Dad is a Volcano. Why? Because Volcanoes erupt most often when and where they feel the safest. Volcanoes may actually be upset at their boss or their child or their pastor, for example, but you end up bearing the brunt of their vengeance because you are safer to get mad at. So, if you find that you are continually the object of a Volcano's eruptions, it is probably because you are a "safe object"— a

Anger blows out the lamp of the mind.
Robert Green Ingersoll

scapegoat. This term comes from the Old Testament reference to the innocent goat that was brought to the altar by the high priest (see Lev. 16:20-22). Laying both hands on the goat's head, the high priest confessed the sins of the people. The goat was then taken out into the wilderness and allowed to go free, thus symbolically taking all the sins of the people into a land that was uninhabited.

Do you ever feel like this goat when you are the object of Volcanoes' anger? It's not uncommon. Usually you are an innocent bystander, doing nothing wrong, when suddenly you become the recipient of anger, heaped on your head like red-hot cinders blasted from a violent mountain. Understanding this common phenomenon can help you cope with Volcanoes in two ways. First, you can take comfort in knowing you are not the cause of this anger. And second, you can set boundaries with these people by helping them identify the true object of their wrath; that way you won't become their scapegoat.

Guard against Contamination

In his autobiography, *Number 1,* former New York Yankees manager Billy Martin tells about hunting in Texas with baseball star Mickey Mantle at his friend's ranch. When they reached the ranch, Mantle told Martin to wait in the car while he checked with his friend. Mantle's friend quickly gave them permission to hunt, but he asked

Mantle a favor. He had a pet mule who was going blind, and he didn't have the heart to put him out of his misery. He asked Mantle to shoot the mule for him. When Mantle came back to the car, he pretended to be angry. He scowled and slammed the door. Martin asked him what was wrong, and Mantle said his friend wouldn't let them hunt.

> **Men often make up in wrath what they want in reason.**
> William Rounseville Alger

"I'm so mad at that guy," Mantle said, "I'm going out to his barn and shoot one of his mules!" Mantle drove like a maniac to the barn. Martin protested, but Mantle was adamant. "Just watch me!" he shouted. When they got to the barn, Mantle jumped out of the car with his rifle, ran inside, and shot the mule. As he was leaving, though, he heard two shots, and he ran back to the car. He saw that Martin had taken out his rifle too. "What are you doing, Martin?" he yelled.

Martin yelled back, face red with anger, "We'll show that son of a gun! I just killed two of his cows!"

Anger can be dangerously contagious. As Proverbs puts it, "Do not make friends with a hot-tempered man . . . or you may learn his ways" (Prov. 22:24-25).

Consider a Hassle Log

If the Volcanoes in your life admit that they have a problem with anger and are open to working on it, you might suggest that they keep a "Hassle Log." This is a technique I often use with angry clients I am seeing in therapy, but it doesn't take a professional to make good use of it. The hassle log is a diary-like means of analyzing provocative events. Volcanoes keep a record of all their anger, including places, happenings, persons present, what they did or said, the results, how they felt afterward, and what they wish they had done differently. This simple exercise heightens Volcanoes' awareness of where, when, why, and how often they get angry. And this awareness can do more than you imagine to help Volcanoes keep their cool. Keeping a hassle log for just a week could be a major turning point in their life and yours.

Leave Room for God

A Volcano coworker blows into your office and reprimands you for something about which you had no responsibility. The Volcano shouts loudly about your incompetence as you stare in utter disbelief. As the Volcano leans toward you over the desk and points a finger in your face, you feel your blood begin to simmer. What do you do next? Do you lunge at the Volcano in self-defense and scream, "You are out of line"? If not, you might at least dream of doing something so dramatic. It is only natural to fight back when we are attacked. It is only natural to want justice and serve punishment. But the truth is that getting angry at Volcanoes is a deadly drama. No one wins when that's the game. Instead, you should do everything within your power not to pay back their anger with more anger. God has laid down this important principle for us, and the apostle Paul emphasizes it in his letter to the

> **Whenever you are angry, be assured that it is not only a present evil, but that you have increased a habit.** Epictetus

Romans: "Never pay back evil for evil. Let your aims be such as all men count honourable. If possible, so far as it lies with you, live at peace with all men. My dear friends, do not seek revenge, but leave a place for divine retribution" (Rom. 12:17-19 NEB). That's the key: Leave all punishment to God.

Surrender Your Right to Hurt Back

My academic mentor in graduate school was Dr. Archibald Hart. He is a godly man who cared a lot about my character and, among many other things, taught me how to handle anger when I felt like fighting back. "Les," he would say, "never forget to forgive." And he would remind me of Paul's writing in Ephesians: "Have done with spite and passion, all angry shouting and cursing, and bad feeling of every kind. Be generous to one another, tender-hearted, forgiving one another as God in Christ forgave you" (Eph. 4:31-32, NEB). Forgiveness, Dr. Hart would say, is surrendering my right to hurt you back if you hurt me. I like that definition. It means that when I am the object of anger I don't deserve, I can choose to forgive the Volcano by not trying to strike back. In this sense, forgiveness leaves room for God to mete out retribution, not me. So rid yourself of angry shouting, and surrender your right to hurt back.

Don't Go to War without Understanding the Battle

If you find yourself unwittingly caught in an angry tug-of-war with Volcanoes who erupt without warning, don't pull out all of your artillery before you clearly understand what you are fighting for. This is how irreparable damage is done to relationships and families. Instead, postpone your urge to prove your point, and take the time to define clearly what the battle is about. Say to Volcanoes: "I want to be sure I understand what is upsetting you. Is it that . . . ?" By defining the conflict, you bring some objectivity into it and can avoid a lot of useless strife. Dr. Carol Tavris, author of *Anger: The Misunderstood Emotion,* advises: "Never speak in the heat of anger. You say things badly or wrongly. Give yourself time to cool off because you want your anger to accomplish something."

Keep cool; anger is not an argument.
Daniel Webster

Appreciate the Contribution Volcanoes Make

When a destructive trait like anger colors people's demeanor, it is easy to lose sight of their positive traits. In trying to cope with Volcanoes, I often remind myself that even geological volcanoes offer great benefits (despite their destructive power). For example, many volcanic materials have important industrial and chemical uses. Rock formed from lava is commonly used in building roads. Weathered volcanic ash greatly improves soil fertility. In many volcanic regions, people use underground steam as a source of energy. For scientists, volcanoes serve as "windows" to the earth's interior. You get the idea: Just as geological volcanoes offer many benefits, so do human Volcanoes. So take some time to identify the positive qualities in the Volcanoes in your life. It will help you cope more effectively with intermittent, emotional explosions.

CROSS-REFERENCE

For more information related to Volcanoes, see these other high-maintenance relationships: the Cold Shoulder, the Critic, and the Steamroller.

12

THE SPONGE

Constantly in Need but
Gives Nothing Back

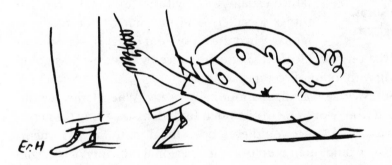

SHORTLY after moving into a new building, Melissa knocked on the door of the apartment across from hers. That's where she met Janice. "Hi, I'm Melissa, your new neighbor. I know this sounds ridiculous, but I just can't figure out how to set the air conditioner in my apartment."

The two women hit it off right from the beginning. They had a lot in common; both were single and in their late twenties. One difference, however, was that while Janice had a full-time job with an ad agency, Melissa had only a part-time job at a florist (not because she had to, but because she liked flowers) and was supported mostly by a trust fund. Still, the two women became good friends. As the relationship progressed, Janice was drawn to Melissa's disarming sense of helplessness.

You see, Melissa not only didn't know how to set her air conditioner but also had trouble finding her way around the city, deciding what restaurant to go to, knowing how to get the oil changed in her car, which shoes matched which dress, and on and on. And without her really knowing it, all this neediness became attractive to Janice. She liked the way she felt around Melissa—more competent, more needed, and more appreciated.

Janice and Melissa began spending a great deal of time together. But gradually, the relationship became imbalanced, with Janice carrying most of the weight. On one occasion, Janice tried to get Melissa to become more independent. She got in touch with a few friends and lined up some job interviews for her. She lent her a jacket. Then Melissa remembered the gorgeous ecru blouse Janice usually wore with it. "You really can put things together," she murmured admiringly as Janice fished the blouse out of her closet. Melissa thrived on being looked after, and Janice by this time was going along with it out of common courtesy.

> **The man who lives by himself and for himself is likely to be corrupted by the company he keeps.**
> Charles H. Parkhurst

But Melissa was also emotionally needy. When Janice would return from work, she would often find Melissa waiting for her to arrive. Before Janice could even open the door to her apartment, Melissa would often blurt out some personal difficulty or struggle. These after-work talk sessions eventually turned into standing invitations for dinner, and before she even knew it, Janice was constantly supplying free help, advice, and consolation (not to mention food)—and Melissa was soaking it up.

After months of helping Melissa make decisions and after months of listening to her struggles, Janice realized that she had become Melissa's unofficial caretaker. Their relationship was not based on mutual sharing. It was based on Janice giving and Melissa receiving.

Do know people like Melissa, people on the helpless, needy side? Do you know people who require more attention than you get in return? If so, you know the realities of relating to Sponges.

You know what it is like to sit with these people through tedious, self-deprecating conversations and patiently listen to their struggles. You know what it is like to be with people who are constantly in need but who rarely, if ever, give anything in return.

You may also know that these human Sponges can exhaust you, drain you, and suck the life right out of you. What you may not know is that you don't have to be a victim of these bottomless pits of need. You can practice genuine friendship and true compassion without feeling like an unpaid nursemaid. This chapter will show you how.

THE ANATOMY OF A SPONGE

Marine biologists tell us that as many as five thousand different varieties of sponges live at the bottom of oceans. There may be as many styles of human Sponges too. But while all Sponges have their own unique characteristics, several traits are common to most of them. Sponges are clingy, stifling, needy, guilt-inducing, fearful, egocentric, smothering, and crisis-oriented.

Clingy

"I was at a party with my friend," confessed James, "and she wouldn't leave my side even after I told her I wanted to mingle. In fact, that's when she ran out in tears." James encountered one of the sure signs of human Sponges—being clingy. They attach themselves to you and hang on for dear life.

Stifling

In healthy relationships two people grow and develop because of the relationship. But mutual development doesn't happen in relationships with Sponges. Sponges tend to stifle the life out of relationships.

Needy

Sponges are often broke. They're frequently looking for a better job. They need a new car. They're down on their luck. They need, well, they need a lot. That's a defining mark of Sponges. Without needs, they have no way to get close to others, so they plague you for advice on matters both large and small.

Guilt-Inducing

Sponges are experts at making you feel horribly guilty if you don't offer to help them. "I'm so worried my plants will die while I'm in Boston next month," they might say. The only human response to a statement like this is, "Ooooh! Let me water them!" If you don't, you feel like a heel.

Fearful

On a recent trip to Singapore I learned a new term: *kiasu*. At a conference where I was speaking, people were eagerly buying books. They could not get them quickly enough, and many people seemed to buy the books without even looking at the covers. I mentioned this to the person overseeing the book table, and he said, "Oh, that's *kiasu*, a Chinese fear of losing out on what others have." Sponges have the same fear. They don't want to miss out, and they are counting on you to be sure they don't.

Egocentric

It sounds rather blunt, but it's the truth: Sponges are egocentric, always looking out for themselves. They are consumed by their own needs and can't look beyond them. They are more concerned with how they are feeling and how they are doing than they are with anything else. Sponges, while not necessarily selfish, are certainly egocentric.

Smothering

In healthy relationships, closeness ebbs and flows. The relationship has a kind of center point where people are connected, but they move closer and farther away from this point over time. Most people understand this and learn to tolerate the periods of greater distance without panicking. But not Sponges. They panic when they sense distance, so they smother and hover in a typically vain attempt to stay close.

Crisis-Oriented

A crisis is what gets some Sponges out of bed in the morning. It fuels them the way coffee fuels other people. "What am I going to do-o-o?" they cry, waiting for you to rush in— with clothes, a bed, a meal, an introduction, a car, your ear. A crisis can bring out the most help from others, and Sponges know it.

DO YOU KNOW A SPONGE?

The following self-test can help you assess whether you are in a high-maintenance relationship with a Sponge. Identify the person or people who have come to your mind as you have read the preceding paragraphs. Circle the *Y* if the statement is true of the person or people about whom you are thinking. Circle the *N* if the statement does not apply to this person or people.

Y N Sometimes I feel that this person is attached to my side.

Y N Rarely does this person explore my needs and concerns.

Y N Sometimes it feels as if this person is literally soaking up my time and resources.

Y N This relationship may be close in some respects, but it is stagnant.

Y N This person almost always appears to be needy.

Y N When I say no to this person, I often feel guilty.

Y N This person is clingy and needy.

Y N I often feel smothered by this person.

Y N It sometimes feels as if this person is simply moving from one crisis to another.

Y N At times I feel as if this person is pulling me under.

Y N This person has a fear of missing out or being left out.

Y N I have difficulty setting boundaries with this person.

Y N I spend a disproportionate amount of time working on this person's problems and concerns compared to my own.

Y N This person is not afraid to ask for a favor.

Y N This person often drains my energy.

Scoring: Total the number of *Y*s you circled. If you circled ten or more *Y*s, you are certainly in a high-maintenance relationship with a Sponge.

UNDERSTANDING SPONGES

Finish the sentence: "If at first you don't succeed . . ." Do you have your response? My hunch is that you said something like "Try again." Not so for Sponges. They are more likely to come up with something like "You are utterly useless." *Sponges suffer from terribly low self-esteem.* In fact, University of Washington psychologist Jonathan Brown put people's self-esteem to the test and shed some light on why Sponges act the way they do.[1] He had a group of 172 people— 81 with high self-esteem, the rest with low— play a computer word game. Half the participants received a version too difficult to do in the time allotted, assuring their failure. Afterward, Brown asked them to evaluate their performance.

For those with low self-esteem, failure hit like the proverbial ton of bricks. Feelings of shame and humiliation rose from their rubble. Worse, they overgeneralized their failure, rating their intelligence and competence more negatively after a poor performance than a successful one.

> Selfishness is the greatest curse of the human race.
> William E. Gladstone

The people with high self-esteem did just the opposite. They rated their intelligence a bit higher after failure, compensating for their performance.

This is the value of self-esteem, explains Brown: It enables us to respond to events—good or bad—in ways that bolster our sense of worth.

Sponges, suffering from unrealistically low self-esteem, agonize over their failure and as a result are far less willing to take risks and far more apt to rely on others. Jesus told a parable about a Sponge, a person with self-esteem so low that he buried his talents in the ground (see Matt. 25:14-30). This is the crux of the matter for Sponges: *They don't possess enough self-worth to stand on their own two feet, so they try to stand on yours.*

In this sense, Sponges are desperately trying to merge with another person in a vain attempt to feel better about themselves. This happens even in marriage. When one spouse is too wrapped up in the other partner, the spouse puts the relationship in jeopardy. It creates a symbiotic marriage: If the spouse is sad, the Sponge is sad; if the spouse is happy, the Sponge is happy. That may not sound too bad, but problems arise when Sponges can't tell where they end and their spouse begins. The relationship becomes too close for comfort.

Sponges are needy because their neediness serves as a bridge to other people. It is their way of getting closer to other people. It's a little deceptive because their neediness is not so much about getting their overt needs met as it is about something deeper. *Sponges, more than most other high-maintenance relationships, are crying out, strangely enough, to be needed.*

COPING WITH SPONGES

Were you ever taught to say no? I wasn't. In fact, in most "good" homes, saying no signaled that we were (gasp) selfish, the worst sin of all. Am I right? If you identify with this inner tug to let Sponges take control because you are a "good" person, then take a deep breath. Relax. You don't have to enter rehabilitation for being a "yes addict." Of course, saying no is important to cop-

> **What I gave, I have; what I spent, I had; what I kept, I lost.**
> Old epitaph

ing with Sponges, but there are plenty of other proven strategies for not allowing Sponges to soak up every ounce of your time and energy. Here's how.

Face the Sponge Within

Maybe you are repulsed by the constant neediness of Sponges. Perhaps you are put off by their guilt-inducing ways. Maybe you are sickened by the way they drain you of time, energy, and resources. But in spite of your understandable feelings, a good place to start coping with Sponges is by identifying the parts of *you* that are similar to them. I'm not saying you are the kind of person to ask friends if you can move into their apartment for three weeks while your place is getting painted. I'm not suggesting you would dump your personal problems on other people without giving them the emotional support they need too. But I am suggesting that at times you also feel a need to have someone to care for you. It may not be strong, and it may only be fleeting, but it is a need just the same. If you can own up to a part of the Sponge in you, then you will be more likely to give more grace to the Sponges around you.

Examine Your Desire to Help

"I always play therapist to my friends and get zero in return," griped Ellen to her husband. He responded by telling her that she never seems to *want* anything in return. At that moment, Ellen realized she had set a precedent for always listening and never being listened to. Why? Because it played into her compulsive need to help. Ellen, like so many people relating to Sponges, had fallen into what counselor Carmen Renee Berry calls the "Messiah Trap."[2] This is a trap set by the lie "Everyone else's needs are more important than mine." The truth is that your needs are critically important. If you do not identify your own needs, you will have trouble accurately meeting the needs of others. So if you hear that lie reverberating in your brain from time to time, I challenge you to do a simple exercise. Make a list of your own needs and desires. Be intentional about it. On a piece of paper, write down whatever comes to mind. The point is to acknowledge that you have vulnerabilities too, that Sponges don't have a monopoly on needs. Yours are just as real. Once you accept this, you can loosen up your compulsion to give and learn to build more balanced relationships, in which you also receive.

> For anything worth having one must pay the price; and the price is always work, patience, love, self-sacrifice—no paper currency, no promises to pay, but the gold of real service.
> John Burroughs

Clean Out the Clutter of Sloppy Agape

In his book *Maverick*, Ricardo Semler tells of a powerful lesson he learned working at Semco, a large corporation. He was in a meeting in which the purchase of $50,000 worth of file cabinets was proposed. Several departments had been waiting months for the cabinets, and in desperation they decided to pool their requests. "We didn't buy a single new file cabinet that day," Semler writes. "Instead we decided to stop the company for half a day and hold the First Biannual File Inspection and Clean-out." The administrators gave simple instructions for everyone to look inside every file folder and purge every nonessential piece of paper. "I was one of Semco's biggest file hogs, with four large cabinets and a request for two more," said Semler. After the cleanup, however, he had trimmed down to a single cabinet. The same was true for many other employees. In fact, the cleanup went so well that when everyone had finished, Semco auctioned off dozens of unneeded file cabinets.

The same lesson can be applied to relationships with Sponges. Sometimes what we think we need to give to them isn't what they really need. So pray for discernment, and clean out the clutter of the relationship, the excesses of compulsive compassion that are not managed by healthy boundaries. Pare down to the essentials of how you can be most helpful, and clean up your "sloppy agape."

Deflate the Crisis

In the midst of yet another crisis, Wendy dropped by Karen's place just as Karen was leaving for work. "I've got to be out of here in five minutes," Karen told her.

"I can't believe what it was like at my folks' place," Wendy groaned. "I couldn't take a shower . . . only cold water."

"That's terrible," Karen said.

"I'm filthy," Wendy responded.

Now it was Karen's turn. Wendy was waiting for her to say, "Here's a nice fluffy towel. I just cleaned the bathroom. Come take a long hot shower. Make sure you lock the door on your way out."

This time, however, Karen responded differently. "You'll think of something," she said. "You always do." With that, Karen walked toward her door to leave for work.

What Wendy was asking and what Karen was denying was implicit. But after that incident, Wendy stopped testing what Karen would do for her, and Karen feels much better about the friendship.

Accept the Bottomless Pit of Needs

One of humorist Erma Bombeck's favorite Jewish grandmother stories concerns a grandson who went to the beach with his grandmother. The boy carried his bucket, shovel, and sun hat. As he played in the sand near the shore, the grandmother dozed off. As she slept, a large wave dragged the child out to sea. The grandmother awoke and was devastated. She fell to the ground on her knees and prayed, "God, if you save my grandchild, I promise I'll make it up to you. I'll join whatever club you want me to. I'll volunteer at the hospital, give to the poor, and do anything that makes you happy." Suddenly, her grandson was tossed onto the beach at her feet. The boy was alive! But as the grandmother stood up, she seemed to be upset. She put her hands on her hips, looked skyward, and said sharply, "He had a hat, you know."[3] Sponges are a lot like that grandmother. They appear so urgent and so needy. But when you try to fill their need, they seem never to be satisfied. Get over the surprise (and the giving) and realize that for true Sponges, no matter how much you give, they will still want more.

Say No, and Don't Feel Guilty

Saying no is an art. It is a tool for governing your time and energy so that you can see yourself clearly in relation to the rest of the world. Saying no is also the linchpin of staying healthy in relation to Sponges. It lets you weed out what is unnecessary, inappropriate, or just conflicting. For example, a Sponge needs money for a trip home to attend an old friend's wedding. What do you say when she asks you for financial help? Saying yes would mean using money you have been saving for a long-planned trip. Do you say no? If you do, are you likely to pummel yourself with guilt? You don't need to. You are under no obligation to give in to a request, regardless of how persuasively it is made. As the expression goes, just because you *can* doesn't mean you *should*.

> **The avaricious man is like the barren sandy ground of the desert which sucks in all the rain and dew with greediness, but yields no fruitful herbs or plants for the benefit of others.** Zeno

The rule I try to live by is not to accept anything as my obligation until I've first embraced it as my commitment. This takes guilt out of the equation. You see, whenever you assume an obligation knowing you don't have the resources or the time or the commitment to live up to it, you verge on being a Martyr (and everyone knows how much fun these high-maintenance people are). So try it out. Say no gracefully by thanking the person for thinking of you, and then explain your circumstances if you need to. But remember, it really is possible to say no and not feel guilty.

Turn Sympathy into Empathy

Henry Ford said, "If there is any one secret of success, it lies in the ability to get the other person's point of view and see things from that person's angle as well as from your own." I couldn't agree more. What he is talking about is empathy—that artful ability to put ourselves in another's skin with both our heart and head. Of course, that is the trick: *both* heart and head. Too often we confuse empathy with feeling another's pain in our heart. But that's only sympathy. And while sympathy is a noble expression, it is only half of what it takes to have empathy. Empathy adds to sympathy an objective sense of analyzing

> **If the light is red or even yellow, you're wise to let God hold you back.**
> Charles Swindoll

people's problems before getting worked up over them. And that's one of the keys to coping with Sponges: to analyze as well as sympathize. So take time to be objective about Sponges' circumstances before you jump "heart first" into helping them. If you do, you will turn sympathy into empathy and help yourself as well as the Sponges in the process.

Build Good Boundaries

In my work as a medical psychologist on a hospital burn unit, I have spent countless hours working with families who would do just about anything to help their family member who is suffering. But before I discharge a burn patient into the care of a family like this, I tell the family members, "Set good boundaries. During the patient's first day home, don't do anything that you are not prepared to do for the rest of your life." I have seen too many families make "temporary" changes that become permanent patterns of pleasing.

We need to build the same kinds of boundaries in our relationships with Sponges. You may think that allowing a Sponge to sleep on your couch for a night would really help out. But after this offer becomes a standing invitation several times a month, you realize that it is more than temporary. That's when it's time to set boundaries— clear, objective rules that both you and the Sponge understand.

The best way to understand where you need to set boundaries

is to think about the people whom you have worked hardest to help. Note what kinds of behavior triggered your urge to make them happy, and consider ways of keeping your urge to please under control. Then set up your expectations, make them known, and stick to your guns. If you are willing to loan your car to a Sponge, for example, decide how often and how many times. Say, "This is what I can do for you, but no more."

Confront When Necessary

One of the most common and dangerous mistakes you can make in relating to Sponges is to allow steam to build up within yourself because you are not confronting the annoyance. If you do this, you will eventually explode. You may end up shouting, "You always talk about yourself, and you're driving me nuts!" A far better strategy is to confront the Sponges about how they are making you feel. Confrontation is always risky, but it is much safer than letting your frustration run rampant. Think of confrontation as holding up a mirror to help Sponges see what they are doing and how it is affecting you. It is possible they have no idea that they are dumping on you or that you feel they never listen. It is possible they assume that because they talk so freely about their problems, you'll jump in and talk about yours too. Salvage what you can from this high-maintenance relationship by gently communicating what you see taking place. It may be the most loving thing you can do for the Sponges in your life.

> **However far you go, it is not much use if it is not in the right direction.**
> William Barclay

CROSS-REFERENCE

For more information related to Sponges, see these other high-maintenance relationships: the Chameleon, the Green-Eyed Monster, and the Martyr.

13

THE COMPETITOR

Keeps Track of Tit for Tat

THE desert sun is on the rise and already packing a punch only a lizard could love. It would be 99 degrees in the shade, if there were any. The acres of hot, outdoor tennis courts at the Mission Hills tennis complex are deserted, except for one. On its simmering surface is a teenager whacking tennis balls across the net as fast as her male sparring partner can deliver them. She burns one double-barreled backhand after another beyond his reach.

The teenager happens to be Jennifer Capriati, who turned pro at age thirteen and was once touted to be "the next Chris Evert." But little more than three years after becoming the youngest player ever to rank in the top ten and after passing the $1 million mark in career earnings at Wimbledon and after winning a gold medal at the Olympic Games in Barcelona, Jennifer, the consummate competitor, hit bottom.

Suffering a destabilizing loss at the 1993 U.S. Open, Jennifer cried incessantly and eventually crawled over the edge of an emotional precipice and fell into a self-destructive limbo that resulted in, among other things, being cited for shoplifting and being arrested for drug possession. For several months Jennifer had residual nightmares about losing. "I spent a week in bed in darkness after that, just hating everything," she later told reporters. "When I looked in my mirror, I actually saw this distorted image: I was so ugly and so fat, I just wanted to kill myself, really." What Jennifer did kill was her public self. She turned her back on tennis, dropped out of competition, and refused to touch a racquet for months.

> **Nothing is ever done beautifully which is done in rivalship.**
> John Ruskin

Jennifer sums up her downward spiral by saying: "The way I felt about myself had to do with how I played, and if I played terrible I'd say, yes, I can handle it, but really I couldn't; I felt like no one liked me as a person." In a moment of real vulnerability, she confessed: "I was always expected to be at the top, and *if I didn't win, to me that meant I was a loser.*"

In a single sentence, this young tennis star cuts to the core of what it's like to be consumed by competition. For Competitors — whether in sports or anything else—winning is everything and losing is disastrous.

Most of us like a little friendly competition now and then, but Competitors don't know when to stop. They turn practically every activity, on or off the court, into a contest, replete with awards, trophies, and rankings. Anything and everything becomes an opportunity to outwit and surpass you—from making a reservation at a restaurant to getting married to waking up in the morning. It's all about competition. If you tell Competitors a story about how great your vacation was, they will tell you how much better theirs was. One point for the Competitors. Tell them how hard you worked today, and they will surpass your story by telling you about their double-booked calendar and their endless stream of appointments. Two points for the Competitors. That's how the game is played —by keeping score.

Of course, Competitors are found not only at work or in social circles. Very often they live in our homes. What brother or sister, for example, cannot tell the story of unremitting jealousy and competition? Even into adulthood, sibling rivalry rears its head from time to time. But for Competitors, it never leaves. For them, even Christmas becomes a contest: their gifts reveal that they truly are more devoted children.

The telltale sign of true Competitors, whether they are coworkers, friends, or relatives, is that they think the only interesting conversation is a game of "try and top this." And even though you're aware of their ploy, you always find yourself trapped in a useless game, competing for . . . well, competing for competition's sake. And you almost always feel like a loser.

THE ANATOMY OF A COMPETITOR

Competitors rarely fit into a prescribed profile or mold. However, in general, people that are consumed by competition are usually ambitious, envious, relentless, individualistic, legalistic, flamboyant, strategic, intimidating, and punitive.

Ambitious

"It's a jungle out there," say the Competitors, "a dog-eat-dog world where the only rule is survival of the fittest." There is no lackadaisical attitude of simply hoping for the best here. Competitors have a tiger in their tank, an unquenchable ambition driving them to pursue whatever is just out of reach. You don't have to hunt for the tiger either. Competitors will be the first to tell you that they are moving up, that they have their sights set on something big. They are climbing the ladder to the top and weighing every situation in terms of what it can do to advance their standing.

Envious

Envy is not a gentle emotion. It's not just "I want what you have." It's an aggressive "I want what you have, and I want you not to have it. I want to take it away from you, and if I can't do that, I'll spoil it for you." Competitors are prone to envy rather than jealousy, which is more civilized and focuses on possessing what someone else has or does and thus removes the rivalry. Envy, on the other hand, is competitive by comparison, focusing on what others have and what they themselves lack.

Relentless

Competitors rarely relax and almost never give up. Like tenacious pit bulls, they relentlessly hold fast to their pursuit. Competitors don't understand that competition has a way of draining the playfulness from any activity—sports, music, even conversation. Losing isn't fun, and in most competitions, more than half of the competitors lose (consider the many applicants for a single job). In fact, in many cases, Competitors "win" because they simply wear their competition down.

Individualistic

To compete means to strive for something for which others are also contending. By definition, Competitors are individualists. "Me against the world" is their theme. They are rarely team players, and they view relying on others as a sign of weakness. As rugged individualists they hold true to their call: Do it the easy way; don't ask for help.

Legalistic

I know a Competitor who studies proper English just to catch people making a grammatical mistake. He phoned me the other day and asked how I felt about an important presentation. "I think I did good," I replied.

"Did good?" he squealed with delight. Confused, I asked what was so funny. "Good! You said 'good' instead of 'well'—I got you!" Nothing makes this fellow feel better than one-upping someone on insignificant, legalistic points.

Flamboyant

Competitors tend to gloat about their achievements, past and present. They try to impress you with what they have done. When it comes to their parenting skills, for example, they have no problem listing the achievements of their children and telling you just how great they are. This kind of grandstanding is their way of letting you know they are a contender and that you need to beware of their proficiency if you decide to take them on.

Strategic

For the most part, Competitors do not shoot from the hip. They come prepared, having practiced their moves and memorized their plans. Like all-star quarterbacks, Competitors have their playbooks from which they carefully select a strategy for finding their opponent's weak spot and gaining advantage. I spoke with a student who told me that he always tried to ask his roommate a favor just before he fell asleep. "He's more agreeable when he is tired," he told me, "and much more likely to do what I want."

Intimidating

Remember the best-selling book *Winning through Intimidation?* The title sums up a major philosophical tenet held by most Competitors. Looking for any tool to give them an edge in their unending quest to reach the top, savvy Competitors often resort to using intimidation. After all, as any professional boxer will tell you, it is a way of keeping your challenger off guard. So Competitors will use nonverbal behavior, such as a daunting look or gesture, to let you know who has the upper hand.

Punitive

Competitors are sore losers. I was waiting for a flight in the Denver airport recently and noticed a boy who must have been around twelve years old. He was wearing a red T-shirt that proclaimed: "If you come in second place, you are the first loser." I don't know if he understood the impact of his shirt's message, but if he did, he must certainly be a Competitor in training. Competitors despise losing and will blame anything and everything for not coming in first— including themselves. When Competitors do not win, they lose not only the "game" but also a part of themselves. Their very identity is shaken. As Brooklyn Dodgers manager Leo Durocher is known for saying, "Show me a good loser, and I'll show you a loser."

DO YOU KNOW A COMPETITOR?

The following self-test can help you assess whether you are in a high-maintenance relationship with a Competitor. Identify the person or people who have come to your mind as you have read the preceding paragraphs. Circle the *Y* if the statement is true of the person or people about whom you are thinking. Circle the *N* if the statement does not apply to this person or people.

Y N When I am with this person, I often feel that I am trying to impress him or her.

Y N This person rarely, if ever, asks for my help.

Y N This person is desperately trying to climb the ladder of success.

Y N This person can be frustratingly nitpicky.

Y N I sometimes think this person would feel good if I had to suffer.

Y N This person often talks about recent and past personal accomplishments.

Y N Most people agree that this person is a hard worker.

Y N This person hardly ever celebrates my successes, and when he or she does, it doesn't sound genuine.

Y N This person loves any and every competitive event.

Y N This person will often point out little mistakes I make just to let me know he or she is noticing.

Y N It feels as if a scoreboard is attached to our relationship.

Y N If this person doesn't win, he or she suffers great emotional pain for longer periods than most people.

Y N This person almost never reveals a weakness.

Y N Sometimes just being around this person wears me out.

Y N This person seems to enjoy intimidating other people.

Scoring: Total the number of *Y*s you circled. If you circled ten or more *Y*s, you are certainly in a high-maintenance relationship with a Competitor.

UNDERSTANDING COMPETITORS

"What causes fights and quarrels among you?" asks the apostle James. "Don't they come from your desires that battle within you? You want something but don't get it" (James 4:1-2). James surely puts his finger on the key to understanding Competitors. They *have* to win because they want something they never achieve—to quiet the "desires that battle within." *More specifically, Competitors gain their sense of self-worth through competition.* And who can blame them? Our society often equates winning with being worthy.

There is an island in the South Seas where competition is unheard of. They play a game, for example, where a team tosses horseshoes and gets a certain score, but the other side then tries to get the same number of hits. Both sides keep tossing until they reach an exact tie. The goal of the game is not to win but to draw. No winners, no losers, just happy kids.

Surprisingly enough, cooperative endeavors like this are common in many societies around the world, but they are alien to most Americans. As children we learn to win (or lose) by playing games like dodgeball, football, and hockey. Even party games like musical chairs are a brutal competition where one player wins and everyone else loses. Indeed, *we play the games we do because our culture values and celebrates competition* while inhabitants of some Pacific islands play the games they do because their society values and celebrates cooperation.

The only competition worthy of a wise man is with himself.
Washington Allston

Competition is a fact of life for most of us. We grew up hearing Green Bay Packers coach Vince Lombardi's slogan, "Winning isn't everything; it's the only thing." In many of our jobs we are pitted against one another, and a company's success (not to mention our country's) is often attributed to its competitive spirit. Some people, however, carry this competitive attitude into *everything* they do. Such is the story of Competitors.

Most of us enjoy engaging in a little competition within a defined arena; it's something we can turn on and off. We might compete aggressively on the racquetball court at the gym, for example, but we don't mistake driving home on the interstate for racing at the Indy 500. This isn't the case for Competitors. They experience competition as an all-consuming, pervasive, out-of-control obsession.

While Competitors may masquerade as healthy American sports enthusiasts, their relentless drive to compete is far from healthy. Why? Because competition always involves a reference to others: If you win, someone else loses. And nobody likes being a loser. Especially Competitors!

Competitors can reduce normally competent, rational human beings to raw bundles of aggression, hurt, and annoyance— often in a matter of minutes. It happens in many arenas. At work, Competitors aggressively contend for promotions and status, climbing over others to catch the boss's eye. At social gatherings and with friends, Competitors contend for attention, affirmation, and respect. They want to be seen as the best-looking, most-engaging, or smartest guest. But Competitors' most wrenching rivalries are closer to home. The competition between mothers and daughters or fathers and sons is a perennial theme for modern novels and daytime talk shows. And when it comes to brothers and sisters, a third of Americans describe their sibling relationships as lifelong competitions. Have you ever observed two elderly sisters dig at each other's sore spots with astounding accuracy, much as they did in junior high? Or have you ever witnessed two older brothers racing for the last piece of chocolate cake at a family reunion, much as they did in grade school? It seems that sibling competition leaves its mark on adult life, affecting the way Competitors interact with people around them. Whether it be with friends, co-workers, neighbors, or spouses, the residue from childhood can trigger a knee-jerk competitive reaction from Competitors.

> To be ambitious of true honor and of the real glory and perfection of our nature is the very principle and incentive of virtue; but to be ambitious of titles, place, ceremonial respects, and civil pageantry is as vain and little as the things which we court.
> Philip Sidney

Consider the biblical account of Jacob and Esau, twins in competition from the beginning: "The babies jostled each other within her" (Gen. 25:22). The first to be born was Esau, and then Jacob "with his hand grasping Esau's heel" (v. 26). The two boys grew up to be men of different temperaments, each one choosing a distinctive way of life. Esau became a skillful hunter and his father's favorite son because he brought him game from the field. Jacob, on the other hand, lived a more sedentary life as a herdsman. He was his mother's favorite. On one occasion, Esau, returning from a hunt, was famished and exhausted. He begged Jacob for some stew and received it only after Jacob, seeing his brother's weakness, talked Esau into giving him his birthright. Jacob ultimately defrauded Esau of their father's blessing. Jacob, even as an adult, never let go of his brother's heel.

Before going too far, it is important to realize that Competitors are not necessarily *born* competing. Anthropologists report about many other societies in which our style of contending is viewed as exceedingly rude and uncaring. But, of course, human beings are not naturally cooperative either. We can and do cut it both ways. Competitors, by most standards, are making a choice. They can't blame their "competitive nature" on genes. *The origin of a high-octane competitive spirit can generally be traced to deep-seated feelings of insecurity.* Competitors are afraid of failure, and because of this fear, they are easily threatened and are thus repeatedly forced to prove themselves worthy.

We grow small trying to be great.
E. Stanley Jones

Competitors are in a precarious position. *They are measuring their achievement not against their personal capability but against everyone else's capability.* This drives them not only to divide and conquer but also to be superior. And that's dangerous because it undermines wisdom and humility. It opens wide the gate to selfish ambition. Consider these words from the New Testament: "Who is wise and understanding among you? Let him show it by his good life, by deeds done in the humility that comes from wisdom. But if you harbor bitter envy and selfish ambition in your hearts, do not boast about it or deny the truth. Such 'wisdom' does not come down from heaven but is earthly, unspiritual, of the devil. For where you have envy and selfish ambition, there you find disorder and every evil practice" (James 3:13-16).

COPING WITH COMPETITORS

What can you do when faced with a cutthroat relationship? What can be done to cope with Competitors? To be sure, you are not going to change them. In fact, the harder you try, the more competitive they often get. So are we simply left to put up with unwanted rivalries? Hardly. You can do several things to keep from getting sucked into needless competition and improve your relationships with Competitors.

Recognize the Competitor Within

Does a part of you enjoy the rivalry you experience with Competitors? Does a part of you like the connection of playing one-up with each other? Whether at work or at home, you probably are participating in some serious competition— because you like it. You may not want to admit it, but the competition might be what's holding your relationship with the Competitor together. Laura Tracy, author of *The Secret Between Us*, states that the "most intense and highly charged relationships exist in the context of competition. . . . But [competition] is a connection that must be kept secret, especially from ourselves." Few of us admit to being competitive, although we have little problem attributing competitiveness to others. If you want to build a better relationship with Competitors, you first have to face the fact that the two of you have something in common: competition. You don't have to broadcast this secret; you need only admit it to yourself.

> **Live in harmony with one another; be sympathetic, . . . compassionate and humble. Do not repay evil with evil or insult with insult.**
> 1 Peter 3:8-9

Don't Forget Competitors' Motivation

Once you have tapped into any desire on your part to maintain a competitive relationship, the next step is to remind yourself why Competitors do what they do. Remember that they are saddled with insecurity. Because winning, from their point of view, is a reflection of their very identity, Competitors are afraid of losing. Competitors are unable to separate who they are from what they do. Thus if they lose, they believe they *are* losers. If, while interacting with Competitors, you keep this primary motivation in mind, if you remember that they are acting out of insecurity, you will be amazed at how much easier it is to accept them and their games. It basically comes down to empathy. By putting yourself in their shoes, by understanding their perspective, you will give them more grace to be who they need to be, and you will be far less vulnerable to their competitive schemes.

Face the Major Myth of Competition

Most of us are convinced that we play and work better when we want to beat out somebody else. We believe that competition leads to improved performance. Competition, we assume, provides that needed edge to put in the extra hour or the extra effort that will make the difference. The truth of the matter is that competition leads to inferior performance. It's true. Striving for self-mastery is what produces the best results. Research has been telling us this for years. In 1978, researchers studied two groups of kids who were asked to make "silly" collages. One group's artistic work was judged by a panel of professional artists to be superior to the other. What was the difference between the two groups? The less creative group was competing for prizes.

The same pattern emerges with adults. Athletes, for example, who pay attention to personal performance goals shoot better and run faster than athletes who concentrate just on beating their opponents. One of the most startling findings comes from a recent study conducted by Janet Spence at the University of Texas, Austin. Dr. Spence found that performance-oriented business executives earned 16 percent more money than those motivated by competition.[1] This makes sense when you consider that businesspeople locked into a competitive mind-set tend to have a greater fear of failure, are content with just winning, and therefore take fewer creative risks and enjoy their work less. The point is that internal motivation, it turns out, is a far more effective incentive than competition.

> **The only thing more disturbing than a friend with a noisy old car is a friend with a quiet new one.**

Check Your Cooperative Quotient

Tufts University professor Alfie Kohn, author of *No Contest*, says, " 'Healthy competition' is a contradiction in terms."[2] He proposes that the "I win, you lose" attitude is never constructive. But not all experts agree. To many people, winning and losing are matters of degree and attitude. They see a difference between constructive and destructive competition, between fair play and dirty tricks. Receiving the Teacher of the Year award is a sign of good work. But you can't justifiably feel pleased about the award if you won it by surreptitiously sabotaging the efforts of your colleagues. Competitors rarely make this important distinction. But *you* can. An important point to remember is that constructive competition allows room for cooperation. The Latin root of the word competition, *competere*, in fact, means "to strive together." And when you compete with an ally, there are no losers. Both you and your "opponent" are really on the same side. In playing golf, for example, you both want to improve your game and have fun. You help pace each other instead of spending your energies looking for your partner's faults.

Don't Play the Game

Let's make this clear: If people want to make every interaction a contest, nothing will stop them. But you don't have to be a victim, and you don't have to engage in the contest. You can simply refuse to play. At lunch one day with a colleague, I casually said something about a book I was reading. "Oh, I read that book months ago when it first came out," he responded. "I always keep my eye out for the latest publications. Go ahead, give me a title, and I bet I have read it." It's silly, but I found myself racking my brain for recent releases to prove him wrong. It didn't matter to me one iota if he made a point of reading recently published books. Good for him! But why did I now find myself trying to prove him wrong? Because he had set the trap, and I had taken the bait.

> Are we driven people, propelled by the winds of our times, pressed to conform or compete? Or are we called people, the recipients of the gracious beckoning of Christ when he promises to make us into something?
>
> Gordon MacDonald

He was looking for a competition, and without ever intending to, I became his opponent. Before long he was quizzing me on whether or not I had read any recent books. "Well, I haven't read that one, but I bought it, and I read a review of it in the *New York Times*." I couldn't believe these words had come out of my mouth. I was actually trying to convince him that I was no slouch when it came to reading what was hot. But the ridiculous turned into the absurd when he reported the score! "Four to two"—he was actually keeping track of who had read more. If Competitors try to engage you in a subtle game of "top this," you can stop them dead in their tracks by saying something like "I'm glad you feel so good about yourself, but this isn't a competition, is it? I'm only wanting to make conversation." This kind of statement almost always puts an end to needless competition. But if the Competitors are veterans and this doesn't work, lay down the rules: "Here's what I'm going to do, and you can do as you like. I simply won't compete."

Practice Simple Economics

Competitors often ask questions like Who has it? How can I get it? and Why do you have it instead of me? They play what most economists call *zero-sum games:* what you win the other person loses. This principle holds that there is only so much to go around and that eventually it will be used up and we will be at zero. Competitors operate out of this principle. Their envy drives them to lose all sense that there is enough to go around. They think, "If you have a bigger piece, then I'm going to have a smaller piece." But keep in mind that much of the best stuff in life is not scarce. In most homes, for example, there is enough parental love for all children. Friendships, ideas, and interests can be shared without anyone losing out. Try to keep this balanced perspective when dealing with Competitors.

> Opposition inflames the enthusiast, never converts him.
> Johann Friedrich von Schiller

Attend to Your Own Goals

When the very best people in any profession talk about their motivation, they often refer to the work itself, rarely to outdoing others. This is not true of Competitors. They are driven by how they compare to the competition. This, of course, leaves little room for resting in the satisfaction of a job well done. For Competitors, a job is never done well unless it surpasses everyone else's work. And that's rare. To avoid this deadly trap yourself, determine what you want to accomplish, and then pursue that goal. Use "winning" only as a temporary marker to judge your progress, not as an end in itself. In other words, don't fall into the trap of comparing yourself to others. The end of that road is not success, only envy and frustration.

Guard against Envy

Competitiveness is a sign of envy. When Competitors launch into their competitive ways, it is often because you have something they want. It may be tangible, like a position, or it may be intangible, such as a personal quality like self-confidence. Whatever it is, you can avoid clashing with Competitors if you do not dangle what they envy in front of them like a carrot they will never grasp. This infuriates Competitors and leaves you wondering why they are always trying to top you. As much as it is within your power, don't flaunt your success, and don't showcase your accomplishments to Competitors. You risk losing any chance of having meaningful relationships with Competitors if they constantly feel threatened by your success. It is in your best interest to guard against it.

Appreciate Competitors' Strengths

Granted, it's often difficult to appreciate the person who seems to have been nursed, weaned, and nurtured on the win-lose concept. But most Competitors do bring some excellent strengths to any relationship. For one thing, they are doers. Competitors do not sit around and watch things happen. If they become challenged in just about anything, they will work to succeed. This can include your relationship. Self-aware Competitors will often work diligently to improve their relationships. Competitors are also strategic and can devise helpful plans and programs to benefit others. The key is getting their competitive energies channeled in the right direction. Many Competitors also love to have fun. In their lighter moments, their competitive nature can be a springboard to playful bantering and memorable joking. Accentuate the positive qualities in the Competitors in your life. Don't let the qualities that rub you the wrong way keep you from enjoying Competitors as friends.

CROSS-REFERENCE

For more information related to Competitors, see these other high-maintenance relationships: the Control Freak, the Green-Eyed Monster, the Workhorse, and the Steamroller.

14

THE WORKHORSE

*Always Pushes and
Is Never Satisfied*

NOBODY saw it coming. Back in the 1950s, with prosperity on the rise and automated machines marching into the workplace, experts warned of an excess of free time. With computers and other gadgets of convenience, Americans thought they were headed into a time of less work and more leisure. Sociologists even founded an institute to prepare for the dangerous glut of leisure time they saw coming.

Society's fortune-tellers couldn't have missed the mark more. Today's workforce puts in tirelessly long and hard hours. In the past fifteen years, the typical adult's leisure time has shrunk by 40 percent —down from twenty-six to sixteen hours a week. The average adult now pumps forty-seven hours per week into work (way above the forty hours per week logged in 1973). And when it comes to professionals and business owners, the numbers jump to fifty-five hours per week.

Work is consuming. We complain about it. We try to avoid it. We call in sick to get out of it. But only a small minority of us say we could do without our jobs, not just because we need the money, but because we like our work. The work-for-money model passed decades ago. The new American worker is motivated by gratification and fulfillment, not just security. Our desire to work, however, has left weekends, the traditional time for leisure and recuperation, to be filled with more work: catching up on chores and errands. In fact, most Americans feel no more rested on Sunday night than they did on Friday.

> Ambition is so powerful a passion in the human breast, that however high we reach, we are never satisfied.
> Niccoló Machiavelli

As much as average people work, it is hard to imagine that some people work more, much more. They are the Workhorses. And for them, work is an intoxicant. They can't live without it. They are addicted.

"Finally, I don't have to let snow keep me from getting to the office," said Kevin. He was showing me his new four-wheel-drive vehicle. It didn't snow that much in Kansas City, but when it did, he didn't want to be stopped. "I used to keep a change of clothes at work and spend the night on a cot if the weather report looked bad," he confessed. "Now, I can sleep in my own bed and still get to work on snowy mornings."

Neither God nor his boss required the intensity and amount of work Kevin insisted on doing. But work was his life. It was his recreation. If he went swimming for thirty minutes after work, he did it so he could have more energy and go back to work after dinner. Kevin drove fast, ate fast, and seldom lingered over a decision. I know people who received statements from his company dated December 25 because Kevin was in his office much of Christmas—"one of the most productive days on the calendar." Kevin wasn't unpleasant; he was just a Workhorse. And it wore me out just watching him.

If you work with someone like Kevin or if you live with a Workhorse, don't despair. This high-maintenance relationship doesn't have to drive you to death.

THE ANATOMY OF A WORKHORSE

Today, over 26 million men and women— nearly a quarter of the labor force — have shifted part or all of their jobs from the office to the home. It is a massive, full-tilt migration. The fantasy is that life gets better and more controlled if we can combine home and office, work and family. But researchers are quickly discovering that Workhorses can make their way to every workstation, whether in an office complex or the corner of a quiet bedroom. What do Workhorses look like? They are tireless, driven, smug, unsatisfied, impatient, perfectionistic, restless, and intimidating.

Tireless

The *whir* of wheels is endless for Workhorses. Their motors never stop. Their engines always run; their batteries always hum. Even when Workhorses are not working on a project, they are working on a project. It nags them, goads them, rarely leaves them alone. Within the psychic boiler room of the Workhorse there is always at least a skeleton crew, and that crew never takes a break.

Driven

Anyone can become a Workhorse, but most often they are found in professional occupations. Professionals like doctors, teachers, lawyers, musicians, and computer programmers are particularly prone to becoming Workhorses. So are pastors, missionaries, and other Christian leaders. Even in the church, it seems, heavy laden Workhorses can't find rest. They are driven to do more, much more, than is expected or needed. And their compulsions spill over onto others. Workhorses often grumble that their colleagues aren't pulling their weight.

Smug

Since most Workhorses are professionals, their lives are based on expertise that most people do not have. All day long doctors and accountants profess that they know certain matters better than others do. They do this in language that is hard for nonprofessionals to understand and difficult to challenge. As Workhorses move up the ladder of success, their unquestioned authority and sense of control increase. Self-reliance and a certain amount of smugness seem to come with the turf. As Workhorses get to the top of the heap, they look down on others.

Unsatisfied

Oscar Wilder once wrote, "In this world there are only two tragedies. One is not getting what one wants, and the other is getting it." He was trying to warn office warriors that no matter how hard they work at being successful, success won't satisfy them. And he is right. Workhorses are always trying to get to the next rung, and because they are rarely content, they spend their lives indefinitely preparing to live.

Impatient

Did you know that, on average, most of us will spend five years of our lives standing in line? We will spend two years trying to return phone calls, eight months opening direct mail, and one year searching for misplaced objects. Well, that may be okay for average people, but it's not for Workhorses. They are in a mad rush to hurry everything along, sometimes doing more than one activity at the same time, rushing through yellow traffic lights, and finishing other people's sentences. Dr. Archibald Hart, my academic mentor, has written that "hurry sickness and its underlying abundance of adrenaline is an addiction as potent and ultimately as destructive as cocaine or alcohol."

Perfectionistic

Workhorses cannot settle for being simply "good enough." They believe they should be perfect parents, perfect spouses, and perfect workers. Their standards are demanding and unrealistic; no one can live up to them. Yet Workhorses try. They are hard on themselves for making any mistake and suffer tremendous guilt for not being better. In almost any project they will single out a small detail that isn't quite right and declare the whole thing a failure.

Restless

Workhorses are happiest when coming down the home stretch of a project. But don't be fooled. They are not looking forward to a celebration or rest; they already have their eyes on the next item on their endless to-do list. Even when Workhorses have downtime, they are restless. "After a handful of dates," a confused man in his late twenties told me, "Julie began to bring work along on our evening adventures. She'd fidget a lot and then start dictating memos into a pocket tape recorder or phone a business associate on her cellular phone when we could have been enjoying the moonlight on my apartment balcony." Workhorses are forever restless.

Intimidating

Bertrand Russell recorded in his essay "Eminent Men I Have Known" that the most impressive public man he ever met was British statesperson William Gladstone, a definite Workhorse with whom once he had an after-dinner drink of port. Russell was seventeen at the time, and Gladstone was eighty. "For a long time we sat in silence; at last, in his booming bass voice," Russell writes, "he condescended to make his one and only remark: 'This is very good port they've given me, but why have they given it to me in a claret glass?' . . . Never again have I felt such terror." Workhorses have a way of making people feel that way.

DO YOU KNOW A WORKHORSE?

The following self-test can help you assess whether you are in a high-maintenance relationship with a Workhorse. Identify the person or people who have come to your mind as you have read the preceding paragraphs. Circle the *Y* if the statement is true of the person or people about whom you are thinking. Circle the *N* if the statement does not apply to this person or people.

Y   N   This person sometimes takes work-related materials (papers, reading, laptop computer) on vacation or to bed.

Y   N   Once this person starts a job, there is no rest or peace of mind until it is finished.

Y   N   This person constantly needs to be doing something.

Y N This person works long days and brings work home.

Y N This person expects perfection of himself or herself and others.

Y N This person has few close friends with whom to share feelings.

Y N This person has a seeming inability to say no to work.

Y N This person seems relentlessly restless.

Y N Many people feel threatened by this person's productivity and matter-of-fact style.

Y N This person will focus on the one little thing that is wrong.

Y N It seems that just as we should be winding down after a long, hard project, this person is gearing up for a new one.

Y N This person tries to do several things at once.

Y N I sometimes get the feeling this person looks down on others and sees them as less competent than he or she is.

Y N This person is extremely time conscious.

Y N I sometimes worry about this person's physical and emotional health.

Scoring: Total the number of Ys you circled. If you circled ten or more Ys, you are certainly in a high-maintenance relationship with a Workhorse.

UNDERSTANDING WORKHORSES

Most of the time my counseling is done over the course of weeks, if not months. Not so with Robert and Teresa, a couple who had dated off and on for about a year. They called for a one-time appointment, a "reality check," as Robert called it. They wanted a quick assessment of their relationship, that's all. I made no promises but agreed to see them.

I soon learned it was Teresa's idea for the appointment, and it didn't take Freud to figure out that Robert was very ambivalent. Teresa, a corporate lawyer, told me that when Robert, a fellow attorney, started dating her, his last-minute cancellations were routine. "For a long time I didn't think much about it," Teresa told me. "We were both on the partner track at our respective firms, so we each understood when emergencies came up. Law is an all-consuming profession." Gradually, though, Teresa began noticing that while she made an effort to set aside valuable time with Robert, he wasn't giving her the same consideration.

The problem wasn't with Teresa, however; the problem was that Robert couldn't live without work. For a short time, we discussed his drive and obsession with work, and Teresa quickly realized this relationship was going nowhere. They both seemed a little relieved to bring this fact into the open, something they both knew at least unconsciously before stepping into my office. In fact, Teresa's final statement on the way out was rather flip: "I guess I'm being replaced by a bunch of legal briefs."

She was right. As I made a few clinical notes, I found myself wondering why this young professional would choose work over an intelligent and engaging woman. The answer, I realized, was straightforward: Robert, a Workhorse, put everything but his job into the background. Work took precedence even over relationships. What made him that way?

Undergirding Workhorses is a feeling of inferiority. In many cases, Workhorses grew up in homes where the parents set high standards and were sometimes strict or critical. During childhood, these Workhorses probably had their self-worth bandied about, and they learned to view themselves conditionally. That is, they learned they could love themselves only if they were successful and perfect.

As a result of their precarious sense of self-worth, Workhorses come to equate who they are with what they do. And with each success (earning good grades, graduating near the top of the class, landing a great job, getting a promotion) Workhorses feel somewhat better, somewhat hopeful, if only for a moment. Unfortunately, their success reinforces a false sense that success is the measure of everything—including the value of a person. Life for Workhorses becomes a balance

> **Ambition is a lust that is never quenched but grows more inflamed and madder by enjoyment.**
> Thomas Otway

sheet of merit and reward. And in the end, they are left wondering about the payoff. They may achieve their dreams, even exceed them, but they will still be asking, Is this all there is?

Year after year, I watch college students pass through my classroom, knowing that they are pursuing a college education not because it deepens their soul and expands their mind but because it enhances their earning power. I fear for their future because they may learn to equate their value with their performance.

Several authors have written about "the impostor phenomenon," in which many successful people feel that their successes are undeserved and that one day people will unmask them for the frauds they are. *For all the outward trappings of success, Workhorses feel hollow inside.* They can never rest and enjoy their accomplishments. They need one new success after another in order to feel that they are okay and to quiet that inner voice that keeps saying, "If other people knew you the way I know you, they would know what a phony you are."

For most people, work is a means to an end, but for Workhorses work is an end in itself. "Meeting my family's material needs" or "doing the Lord's work" become rationalizations for their addiction to push, push, push. It's true. Most Workhorses deny their relentless pushing and defend their work habits as "normal" or even as "a commitment to excellence." Of all the Workhorses I know, none would freely admit that recognition of their achievements (titles, honors, degrees) or a flagging sense of self-worth played a decisive role in stimulating their work ethic. If you ask them to explain their motivation for working so hard, curiously, they will appear quite unprepared for such a question. Their first reply may be that they have never given it much thought. But deep down, they know the major force in their life is the drive for approval and recognition.

Most people would succeed in small things if they were not troubled with great ambitions.
Henry Wadsworth Longfellow

When I was training as a medical psychologist, a well-known, highly respected, and honored scientific thinker gave a heady lecture about "the etiology of schizophrenia" for the hospital interns. I don't remember much of the lecture, but I will never forget what the speaker said near the end of his remarks. He turned off the projector, leaned over the podium, and made a surprising proclamation to the young scholars who filled the small auditorium: "I was asked to speak to you on my most recent findings, and

I have done that. Now let me tell you young doctors what I wish someone would have told me when I sat where you are. You can save yourself unnecessary frustration in the course of your careers if you ask yourself why you are doing what you are doing. For more than thirty years I have struggled and strained to make an impact in my field, and some would say I have." The room was deathly still. "But only recently have I learned that I cannot measure my self-worth by the number of articles I publish or by the number of people who applaud my findings." That was it. He gathered up his lecture notes and sat down. We were stunned. It took time for his message to sink in, but there was no denying that he had touched a nerve with this group of hard-driving students.

> **Come to me, all you who are weary and burdened, and I will give you rest. . . . For my yoke is easy and my burden is light.**
> **Matthew 11:28, 30**

COPING WITH WORKHORSES

A New York company announced the development of a watch that keeps us on track. It has an alarm that plays pleasant music to remind the wearer periodically that time is passing. But if, when the music is played, the wearer does not reset the watch or respond in some way, a second alarm sounds with a recorded voice that says: "Please hurry! Please hurry!" Workhorses, of course, would never need such a frightening gadget. And chances are, you don't either. Just working with or living around Workhorses is enough to instill anxiety and hurry sickness in most of us. What can we do? Thankfully, there are a number of things you can do to handle high-maintenance relationships with Workhorses.

Face the Workhorse Within

Charlie used to get on my nerves because he would set up self-imposed, near-impossible deadlines for projects and then expect everyone involved to push as relentlessly as he did to meet them. It took me a while, but I eventually realized that the reason I found Charlie annoying was because I often did the same thing. It took another coworker to point it out, but when he did, I suddenly had a great deal more patience for Charlie. Sure, he is in many ways more of a Workhorse than I am, but just realizing that I had a capacity to tap into his high-octane ways was enough to help me take an important step toward accepting him as a Workhorse and not let him get under my skin. The point is, many of us have a tendency to drive hard and work impatiently. Once we face this fact, we make room for a helpful dose of empathy—and that is a critical step in coping effectively with Workhorses.

Keep Up When You Can, and Step Back When You Can't

Relating to Workhorses is like riding a bicycle— if you don't pedal forward, you'll fall off. Because workaholism is so deeply ingrained in Workhorses, it is often easiest simply to go with the flow, keeping up when you can, but getting out of the way when you can't. In other words, when you have reached your limit and Workhorses keep pushing you to do more, set your boundary. "I have done all I can do for now on this project," you can say. "If you want something else on this, you will have to look in a different direction. I'm depleted." Give yourself permission to step back and let them go. Don't try to keep up when you are wiped out. You will only cause aggravation to Workhorses and yourself. Besides, if your job is done, continuing to be busy doesn't make you more productive. I was reminded of this on a recent trip to Paris, where I discovered a French saying surviving from the cavalry days: "When in doubt—gallop!" The idea is that the more active you are, the better results you will get. Of course, this is a myth— one that Workhorses live by. They believe that the harder they work, the more they get done. Robert Pearse of Boston University has labeled this the "buckets-of-sweat syndrome." No direct relationship can be assumed between hard work and positive accomplishment. The adage "Work smarter, not harder" has its roots in the recognition of this fallacy. In fact, I have known people who work for Workhorses and accomplish more than the Workhorses do, in half the time.

> Perhaps the reward of the spirit who tries is not the goal but the exercise. E. V. Cooke

Remember That It's Okay to Be Human

The high expectations and relentless drive of Workhorses leave little room for error. Dr. David Burns, a Philadelphia psychiatrist, talks about persons "whose standards are high beyond reach or reason."[1]

They strain compulsively and unremittingly toward impossible goals and often expect others to do the same. But don't fall for the lie that says you must be perfect. Those who do face a no-win scenario. Why? Because when you fall short (and you will), you will think, "What a stupid idiot I am; I can't do anything right." Instead, give yourself permission to be imperfect, to be human. I have a friend who loves Moroccan food, and one of the things I have learned from eating in these restaurants with Scott is that the Moroccans have a tremendous way of reminding themselves of their humanity. They surround themselves with gorgeous, big rugs, carefully crafted with unique and special designs. But each of these rugs contains an intentional error! The artisans deliberately weave imperfections into their fine rugs to remind them that no one is perfect. In fact, they believe that even the attempt to be perfect is blasphemous. The errors woven into the patterns of the rugs remind them that humans are only human, and only God is God. That is a great reminder for everyone who works or lives with hard-driving Workhorses.

> **Men tire themselves in pursuit of rest.**
> **Laurence Sterne**

Have Fun— Even If Workhorses Don't

Workhorses have a way of draining every activity, even a vacation, of its fun. What should be a playful occasion— going to an amusement park, for example— becomes a task to conquer. I know a Workhorse who takes his family to Disneyland every year on the day that is supposedly the least crowded. He has a strategy for getting to each amusement with efficiency and a precise plan for every moment. So much for spontaneity. He is the only guy I know who can turn the "happiest place on earth" into a day at the office. Well, if you know or live with Workhorses like this, don't let them steal your fun. Make a point of enjoying yourself in spite of their structure. Learn to laugh at it, if only in secret. Several companies are trying to help Workhorses lighten up. Ben & Jerry's Ice Cream, for example, has a standing Joy Committee with a Grand Poobah. Its goal is to help employees have more fun. They instituted the annual "Tacky Dress-Up Day," complete with plaids, paisley, and polyester. During the busiest time of the summer, the ice-cream company hires masseuses to ease the tension. Odetics, a high-technology robotics firm in

Anaheim, California, sponsors Hula-Hoop contests, bubble-gum-blowing competitions, and telephone-booth stuffings. The authors of *The Hundred Best Companies to Work for in America* give dozens of examples of playfulness and fun in many of today's leading businesses. The point is that if you work with a stuffed shirt, you don't have to be one. Have some fun.

Listen with a Third Ear

Work becomes an anesthetic against emotional pain for many Workhorses. And sometimes it serves as a barrier to keep others out and to avoid having to deal honestly with relationships. This is perhaps the saddest side effect of being a Workhorse. But you can help the emotional anesthesia wear off, and you can open up a guarded spirit if you learn the simple skill of reflective listening. It is so simple, in fact, that you can begin practicing it today. The idea is to listen not just to the words that Workhorses speak but also to the feelings that underlie those words. For example, if a person says, "People just aren't following through on their assignments," a natural tendency is to try and solve the problem. But reflective listening sets problem solving aside, focuses on the feelings behind the words, and says something like, "It sounds as if you are disappointed in your colleagues." A simple reflection like this lets Workhorses know you are listening on a deep level in an attempt to understand them.

For Workhorses, happiness is a mirage that recedes the closer they get to their goal.

And the more you do this kind of listening, the safer you become to Workhorses and the more likely they are to be vulnerable. Few things can help you more in your relationships with Workhorses than listening, not to their words, but to the feelings beneath the words. Reflective listening is like a balm to the hurried spirit. It helps people slow down and eventually get in touch with what is driving them to push so hard. Proverbs says, "He who answers before listening— that is his folly and his shame" (Prov. 18:13). And the New Testament tells us to "be quick to listen, slow to speak" (James 1:19). When it comes to Workhorses, that advice is sound.

Give the Gift of Grace

The success ethic of Workhorses runs a collision course with the gospel of grace. Christ did not come to save those who could succeed by their own striving. He came to save the poor, blind, and naked. The gospel breathes not one word about rewarding the rewardable. It is about giving life to the lost and the dead. And it is about a kingdom whose priorities are inverted: The last will be first, and those who lose their lives will find them. Workhorses have lost sight of God's grace. Even as Christians, Workhorses struggle to accept God's free gift of grace. Workhorses feel they must work to achieve God's grace, to prove somehow that they are worthy. I recently read about a college student who tried to bury garbage in the backyard of a rental house rather than pay for garbage service. What this student didn't know, however, was that garbage service in the Canadian town where he lived was free. Similarly, Workhorses try to dispose of the garbage in their personal lives. They work feverishly to hide what they want to discard, namely their feelings of inadequacy and self-reproach. What they have a hard time realizing is that God provides "free garbage service" to everyone in his kingdom.

Clarify the Pursuit

Many times Workhorses will lose sight of their destination. They get caught up in the urgency of pursuit and productivity and fail to notice the signs that tell them they have already arrived. A pastor once asked a prominent member of his congregation, "Whenever I see you, you're always in a hurry. Tell me, where are you running all the time?"

The man answered, "I'm running after success. I'm running after fulfillment. I'm running after the reward for all my hard work."

The pastor responded, "That's a good answer if you assume that all those blessings are somewhere ahead of you and that if you run fast enough, you may catch up with them. But isn't it possible that those blessings are behind you, that they are looking for you, and that the more you run, the harder you make it for them to find you?" Isn't it possible indeed that God has all sorts of wonderful presents for Workhorses—good food and beautiful sunsets and flowers budding in the spring and leaves turning in the fall—but in their pursuit for happiness Workhorses are so constantly on the go that God can't find them at home to deliver the gifts? Scripture says, "See how the lilies of the field grow. They do not labor or spin. Yet I tell you that not even Solomon in all his splendor was dressed like one of these" (Matt. 6:28-29). And Paul reminds spiritual Workhorses that it is "by grace you have been saved, through faith— and this not from yourselves, it is the gift of God—not by works, so that no one can boast" (Eph. 2:8-9).

Bring the Family into Focus

In his helpful book *Ordering Your Private World,* pastor and author Gordon MacDonald writes: "A driven person is usually caught in the uncontrolled pursuit of expansion . . . rarely having any time to appreciate the achievements to date. They are usually too busy for the pursuit of ordinary relationships in marriage, family, or friendship . . . not to speak of one with God."[2] The compulsive nature of Workhorses can be highly destructive to any relationship. Consider their home life. The spouse and children of Workhorses tend to become angry, frustrated, and depressed because they feel rejected and unloved. The children may engage in harmful behaviors such as drug abuse, sex, or even suicide in an effort to get the attention of Workhorses. Of course, Workhorses don't understand this because they feel they are providing their children with "everything they could ever want." Everything, that is, except the Workhorses themselves. If you live with Workhorses, don't allow them to pay the price of a fractured family. Don't remain silent. Hold up a mirror. Let them see themselves and what their workaholism is doing to you and the children. Be gentle but forthright. And have Workhorses suggest ways they can spend more quality time at home (that means without being on the phone, using the fax, or sitting at the computer).

> **Man looks at the outward appearance, but the Lord looks at the heart.**
> 1 Samuel 16:7

Explore Your Own Dream

In *Seasons of a Man's Life,* developmental psychologist Dr. Daniel Levinson sees middle adulthood as the opportunity to renounce the "tyranny of the Dream" and become successful on more realistic terms. He writes, "When a man no longer feels he must be remarkable, he is more free to be himself and work according to his own wishes and talents."[3] This is a lesson all Workhorses need to learn. Unfortunately, there is little you can do to help them learn it. It is one of life's lessons that must be caught rather than taught.

You can, however, explore your own dream in the presence of Workhorses on the chance that some of the benefits of your own exploration might rub off. Of course, this is doomed for failure unless you are genuine. But your authentic soul-searching can give Workhorses fresh insight. One of the best ways to do this is to ask them for their wisdom and input on your process. Over a cup of coffee, perhaps, tell them about the vision you had when you were young, about how you dreamed of becoming someone special. Maybe the dream was planted by parents or teachers, or maybe it came from your own imagination. Talk about how you hoped that your work would be recognized, that your marriage would be perfect, and that your children would be exemplary. Next, talk about how you are learning what research has proven: that you can never be happy until you stop measuring your real-life achievements against your dream. If you can share this kind of conversation and genuinely invite their feedback, you just may spark an inner quest for Workhorses too.

Show the Attitude of Gratitude
Professional success increases the danger of relying on our own expertise and ingenuity. We forget that any favor accorded us, any big break, comes as much from God's hand as from our own efforts. Ultimately, whatever we do is possible only because of the gifts he first gave us. "In heaven," Robert Farrar Capon wrote, "there are . . . no upright, successful types who, by dint of their own integrity, have been accepted into the great country club in the sky. There are only failures, only those who have accepted their deaths in their sins and who have been raised up by the King who himself died that they might live." This is something Workhorses tend to forget. And while you can't remind the Workhorses in your life of this, you can model it. You can express your gratitude for God's gifts. You can acknowledge your fortunate circumstances. As you do, the Workhorses will see how you don't smugly rely on your own efforts for success. By observing you, they just may join in.

Build a Safety Net

Not everyone who puts in long hours is addicted to work. Some people are inspired and energized by what they do for a living, and their sense of well-being and fulfillment is proof that they are not engaging in self-destructive activity. But for others the diagnosis may be quite different. Either kind of Workhorse can be difficult to handle, but the latter may need to be protected. They are the worker bees whose bodies are in revolt. Their long hours, sleepless nights, and punishing regimen have driven their body to fight back. They feel fatigued but can't relax. Their sleep is fitful, and they often wake with work on their mind. Worse yet, they get out of bed in the middle of the night and plunge into paperwork they brought home. Frequent headaches, stomach-aches, back pains, and ulcers are red flags signaling destructive work patterns. If the Workhorses in your life fall into this category, they are on the road to ruin. "I think the mind is where heart disease begins for many people," says heart specialist Dean Ornish. He should know. For the past several years, this University of California physician has been trying to unplug the clogged arteries of heart patients by making radical changes in their lifestyle. The Workhorses he treats are known as the Type A personality. These Workhorses are susceptible to coronary disease, and they need help. If this sounds like the Workhorses you know, urge them to seek professional medical help.

> **A life spent in constant labor is a life wasted, save a man be such a fool as to regard a fulsome obituary notice as ample reward.**
> George Jean Nathan

Keep Hope Alive

If you are discouraged, take heart. There is hope for Workhorses. Consider this well-known passage from the writings of the apostle Paul: "But all these things that I once thought very worthwhile — now I've thrown them all away so that I can put my trust and hope in Christ alone" (Phil. 3:7, TLB). What was Paul writing about? Surely he wasn't a Workhorse, was he? I think maybe in his early life he had been a Workhorse. He described himself as a "Pharisee of the Pharisees." This is like saying that he was a "doctor's doctor," or a "lawyer's lawyer" or a "preacher's preacher," that among those who were Pharisees, he was a standout. He listed all of his credentials with pride. He had fulfilled all of the traditions expected of Pharisees: he had been circumcised when he was eight days old; he had been born into a family of Jewish purity, of the tribe of Benjamin; he had observed strict obedience to every Jewish law and custom (Phil. 3:4-6). In Paul's early life, he had been a zealot, a definite overachiever.

But Saul the Pharisee was converted on the Damascus road, and the experience changed his life. He even changed his name: Saul the Pharisee became Paul the missionary. The persecutor was now a proclaimer of the Good News. He was still a man of passion, and he was still driven. It was his drive that propelled him to plant churches throughout Asia Minor and to expand the Christian movement. But the difference was this: Paul had a greater balance and a new purpose—to trust and glorify God, not himself. A foundational decision altered his life: "But whatever was to my profit I now consider loss for the sake of Christ. What is more, I consider everything a loss compared to the surpassing greatness of knowing Christ Jesus my Lord, for whose sake I have lost all things. I consider them rubbish, that I may gain Christ" (Phil. 3:7-8).

CROSS-REFERENCE

For more information related to Workhorses, see these other high-maintenance relationships: the Competitor, the Steamroller, and the Control Freak.

15

THE FLIRT

Imparts Innuendoes, Which
May Border on Harassment

You and your husband are driving home from a dinner party when he mentions that woman. "What's-his-name's wife, with the pretty smile" is the way he describes her. As if you needed a description.

"You mean the one who was flirting with every man at the party?" is what you say.

"Flirting?" he says in boyish astonishment. "What do you mean *flirting?*"

That's when you say: "You can't be serious. You don't get it, do you? Are you telling me you didn't even see it?"

"See what?" he says.

"See *her*. You didn't notice how she reached out to touch your wrist to punctuate every inane remark she made? You didn't notice her looking at you every time you opened your mouth, as if you were John Kennedy Jr.? You didn't notice how she reduced you to Silly Putty? You didn't notice she was a flirt?"

You also didn't notice you were shouting. When you get home and are making a cup of tea, your husband gives your shoulders a squeeze and asks if you are doing okay. You feel a little ridiculous. Maybe you overreacted. Maybe she was a nice woman with no ulterior motives, and you misread the signals. Then the phone rings. It's Wendy, a friend who was at the same party.

"Could you believe that woman tonight?" she asks. It's only then that your suspicions are confirmed: She *is* a Flirt.

Flirting, that amorous play and coquettish behavior that traditionally begins a dating relationship, can be downright disconcerting when it is exhibited anywhere else. When a woman flirts with your husband, even innocently, it's a threat, not a compliment. The Flirt has no right to toy with your spouse, even if she is seemingly oblivious to her flirtatious behavior.

But that doesn't matter to Flirts. They smile too much and move too close. They respect no boundaries and do not know when to back off. They see people of the opposite gender as trophies.

But the female Flirt is not alone. Far from it. Men can be Flirts too. And more often than not, the male Flirt's conduct is much more unbecoming. It's more blatant and can border on harassment.

Nita Heckendorn is a rare woman who broke through the "glass ceiling" that blocks female executives from reaching the top levels of American business. From the day she joined National Medical Enterprises, she moved quickly through the male-dominated ranks. By the age of forty-seven, Heckendorn had done so well in her role as strategic planner that she was promoted to executive vice president and was in charge of more than forty-eight thousand employees and a $3.8 billion budget. At age fifty, she set her sights on the last big step: she aggressively sought the job of chief executive.

It would never happen. Heckendorn ran into a high-level barrier of sexual harassment. Male directors repeatedly called her "babe," and one even invited her to sit on his lap at a board meeting.

Was this behavior innocent flirting or sexual harassment? The courts will decide. Just as they did in a case involving the nation's largest law firm. Baker & McKenzie was recently ordered to pay $7.1 million in damages to a secretary who endured the repeated groping and grabbing of a senior partner. The award, believed to be the highest ever paid out for an individual sexual-harassment case, probably would not have been made before the era of Clarence Thomas and Anita Hill. But since the sensational 1991 Senate testimony in which the entire nation watched

> **Flattery is a kind of bad money, to which our vanity gives us currency.**
> François de La Rochefoucauld

Thomas fight off charges that he had sexually harassed his female subordinate, the American workplace has resembled an embattled fraternity house struggling to discern the boundary between sexual civility and salacious misconduct.

Everyone knows it now: What some men consider innocent flirtations, most women consider harassment. Women, of course, have felt this all along. But now we know it for a fact. According to a recent study at Bucknell University, flirting for men is a more serious activity. There's more ego at stake. It becomes sort of a conquest. For women, on the other hand, flirting is more of a playful activity. It's an end in itself, rather than a means to an end.

Whether the person is male or female, the high-maintenance relationship with a Flirt is fraught with mixed messages and misinterpretation.

THE ANATOMY OF A FLIRT
Whether the Flirts you know are mesmerizing your spouse or even harassing you at work, they have several characteristics in common: sly, vain, attention seeking, lonely, seductive, power hungry, and opportunistic.

Sly
J. P. Bolduc was like any other Flirt before he lost his job. Once chief executive officer of a large chemical company, he was noto-

rious for "artfully" tricking women into uncomfortable positions. He greeted female colleagues whom he hardly knew, for example, by pulling them into an unwilling embrace when they moved to shake his hand.[1] Many Flirts have their own secret system for getting what they want.

Vain

As incredible as it may seem, Flirts view their outgoing behavior as something for which you are to be grateful. They are often preoccupied with their appearance and consumed by their own image. Remember Sam Malone on the hit television show *Cheers*? He was the consummate Flirt, filled with himself and bewildered when a woman passed up his charms. Flirts are not just immodest; they can be shamelessly vain.

Attention Seeking

"She is the woman in the shortest skirts and the lowest necklines," a friend tells me about Cindy. "At parties, she is the woman most likely to be found sitting on a lap she didn't come with and didn't plan to leave with either." Cindy, like all Flirts, loves the attention. Any tactics that focus the spotlight on them, including dress, conversation, or behavior are appealing to Flirts.

Lonely

The female Flirt is more likely to confess it: "Without a man who is interested in me, I feel so alone." But the harassing male Flirt is often just as lonely. Albert Einstein once commented, "It is strange to be known so universally and yet be so lonely." Flirts might very well say the same thing. They are likely to feel known but not necessarily understood.

Seductive

Who doesn't want to be liked? We all feel better when we know that other people like us and want to be around us. That's why Flirts can at times be so seductive. They set the trap by tapping into a person's fundamental human need to be needed, and in a vulnerable moment, innocent victims fall in. Flirting, after all, is a high-spirited compliment the sexes exchange.

Power Hungry

"I just feel more alive and important when a new man is finding me irresistible," stated one self-confessed Flirt. Like most Flirts, she believed that capturing hearts was not so much about love as it was about power—power over men and other women. Flirts derive a strange sense of strength from dominating a relationship, if only briefly, with their innuendoes and double entendres.

Opportunistic

Ever felt cornered by a Flirt? If so, it probably wasn't entirely by accident. Flirts have a way of setting you up. "May I join you on your trip to the store?" "I liked what you said in the meeting. Can we talk about your insights over lunch?" They will seize any and every opportunity to get you alone and then test their charms. Potiphar's wife is a good biblical example of a Flirt. She "cast longing eyes on Joseph and said, 'Lie with me.'" Joseph refused. She caught him by his garment, and he left it in her hand as he fled. She then accused Joseph of impropriety! She abused her power by persistently trying to seduce Joseph (Gen. 39). Flirts are often strategic and opportunistic.

DO YOU KNOW A FLIRT?

The following self-test can help you assess whether you are in a high-maintenance relationship with a Flirt. Identify the person or people who have come to your mind as you have read the preceding paragraphs. Circle the Y if the statement is true of the person or people about whom you are thinking. Circle the N if the statement does not apply to this person or people.

Y N Just being around this person makes me feel creepy.

Y N This person often dresses seductively.

Y N This person is happiest when talking to persons of the opposite sex.

Y N This person is starving for attention.

Y N This person has an excessive need to interact with persons of the opposite sex.

Y N I feel that this person sometimes corners me in awkward places.

Y N   This person steps beyond appropriate boundaries.

Y N   This person makes light of sexual-harassment-prevention procedures.

Y N   This person makes suggestive comments.

Y N   This person puts on an appearance of self-confidence.

Y N   I've heard other people comment on this person's unwelcome and inappropriate touching.

Y N   I've caught this person in the act of lustful leering.

Y N   This person is known to tell off-color jokes.

Y N   I feel very protective of my spouse when this person is around.

Y N   This person seems to enjoy the power of being flirtatious.

Scoring: Total the number of *Y*s you circled. If you circled ten or more *Y*s, you are certainly in a high-maintenance relationship with a Flirt.

UNDERSTANDING FLIRTS

Neal, a pastor, was a client I saw early in my clinical training. I was under intensive supervision, and it was a good thing. Neal came to therapy because he was having tremendous difficulty with his wife of fourteen years. Lori was ready to leave him unless he got some help. "I don't know what to do," Neal told me. "She becomes extremely jealous whenever I am around other women. It has gotten to the point that she refuses to go to church with me because she thinks I flirt with women in the foyer."

For several weeks, I worked with Neal on how he could manage his overly jealous wife. She refused to come in, which confirmed in my mind her personality problem, so Neal and I worked one-on-one. With input from my supervisors, I helped him practice different strategies for calming his wife's suspicions. During our seventh or eighth session, however, I told him that we should think about termination. "As long as your wife refuses to come in, I think we have done about as much as there is to do," I told him. He agreed, and we scheduled one final session.

When Neal came for his last session, he appeared tired. "Are you okay?" I asked as I greeted him in the waiting room.

"I didn't get much sleep last night," he replied. "I was up

writing you this letter. Here." He handed me three pages of barely legible script on yellow notebook paper. I looked it over for a moment as we walked down the hall and gave it back to him as we entered my office. "Why don't you read it to me, Neal?" I asked. It took most of the session for him to read and cry through his confession of a homosexual encounter he had with his roommate in college nearly twenty years earlier. It was a onetime experience that he kept secret from even his wife. Neal wept uncontrollably, his shoulders shuddering. "This is why I came to see you in the first place," he said.

Now Joseph was well-built and handsome, and after a while his master's wife took notice of Joseph and said, "Come to bed with me!"
Genesis 39:6-7

Instantly, the puzzle fell into place. Neal's wife wasn't paranoid, after all. But Neal *was* a Flirt. He was compensating for his fear of being a homosexual by flirting with every woman he encountered. It was his way of proving to himself that he was not a homosexual.

The point of this illustration is not that every Flirt is compensating for a fear of being homosexual. *The point is that most cases of overly flirtatious behavior indicate an underlying psychological reason.* In other words, Flirts are not necessarily looking for an affair or even some fleeting fun. Oftentimes they are acting out of a deep insecurity and a need for attention. And being flirtatious is one sure way of seeking it.

"Have I told you how great you look in that dress?" a Flirt asks, standing so close you can feel his breath on your ear.

"Gross!" you say to yourself as you back up. *"What's his problem?"* His problem may be that he is just your basic, everyday sleaze, or maybe he has never felt accepted and appreciated by his mother, or he may be going through a midlife crisis, or the problem may be caused by a myriad of other things. It is hard to tell for sure because flirting isn't always flirting to the one who is doing it. Flirtatious activities are often ambiguous. The problem this man may have, as most Flirts do, is a simple difference of perception. He may not *see* himself as being inappropriately flirtatious.

In most cases, Flirts do not mean to offend. A 1985 study cited by the American Psychological Association found that in the work environment, men are four times more likely than women to think the people with whom they flirt will be flattered by their sexual overtures and four times less likely to predict the object of their flirting will be insulted or put off.

A study at Kansas State University showed a video of a male store manager who was training a female employee. Researchers found that the men watching the tape thought that the trainee was acting far more seductive, sexy, and flirtatious than did the women who viewed the tape. In addition, the men also perceived the trainee as being interested in dating the manager, while the women viewers thought she was simply looking for friendship.

There is something else to understand about Flirts. If they are in a position of power, they are often misusing it. And that is harassment. It is known as "quid pro quo" exploitation, and it occurs when a superior makes it clear that if you want to advance in your job, or not to lose it altogether, you have to date him or her. Flirtation that borders on harassment also occurs, however, when the Flirt is not one's employer. The church, by the way, is not exempt from this kind of behavior. In a doctoral thesis done at Fuller Theological Seminary, 37 percent of the ministers surveyed confessed to inappropriate sexual behavior with someone in their congregation. King David may be the prime biblical example of one who abused power in pursuit of sexual conquest. When he saw Bathsheba, he wanted her. And because he was the king, everyone had to obey his orders.

> **Sex has become one of the most discussed subjects of modern times. The Victorians pretended it did not exist; the moderns pretend that nothing else exists.**
> Bishop Fulton J. Sheen

The casual, impulsive, playful banter between men and women is not always easy to classify. It has a way of escalating and, in some cases, spinning recklessly out of control. But if you are hounded by high-maintenance Flirts at any level, you know the uneasiness and pain they can cause. Here are some ways you can cope.

COPING WITH FLIRTS

If Flirts make sexual advances toward you at work, how do you keep your cool and respond in a professional fashion? If someone suddenly turns on the charm and plays up to your husband or wife, how can you temper the person's amorous tone in a tactful manner? You can do several things the next time Flirts say or do something that makes you feel uncomfortable. Some of the following suggestions apply exclusively to the work setting and others to married life. In either case, you can do several things to handle high-maintenance Flirts.

Face the Flirt Within

Of all the high-maintenance relationships, this may be the one that is the toughest to see in yourself. After all, if you are in this kind of relationship, you are probably repulsed by its offensive and harassing nature. But try to see how you have used flirtatious behavior in your own life. Certainly at some point in your life you have tried to draw attention from someone of the

Only a passionate love of purity can save a person from impure passion.

opposite sex. And of course, that is normal. But remember how good it felt when the other person responded positively? Keep that in mind as you try to cope with the Flirts in your life.

Face Flirting's Serious Side

Perhaps you are thinking, "What's the big deal with a little flirtatious fun?" Maybe you believe there is little harm in flirting back with your pursuer. If you do, you are playing with fire. Flirting is sexual and creates an immediate aura of arousal between two consenting people. This is one of the chief pleasures of flirting. Indeed, biologists have recently discovered that the chemistry between a flirting couple is more than a metaphor. Flirting triggers a series of hormonal and neural changes that typically accompany pleasurable sexual activities. So unless you are flirting with someone with whom you plan to be romantically involved, face the fact that you are flirting with disaster.

Don't Blame Yourself

Too often, victims of Flirts feel they have done something wrong to be treated disrespectfully. If Flirts have been annoying you, you may be asking yourself questions. What did I do to provoke this behavior? Was it something I said? Was it something about the way I was dressed? Should I stop wearing perfume? Should I stop being friendly to people at work? Am I not being a good enough spouse? Even if you have been acting in a strictly professional fashion and even if you have been an ideal spouse, you may be worried and uncertain about whether you are somehow to blame. But, most assuredly, you aren't. Let me put this simply. If you are on the receiving end of flirtatious behavior, don't feel guilty. Don't blame yourself.

Never Allow Yourself to Be Cornered

One of the best protections against Flirts is a preventative practice. Solving the problem with Flirts before it even begins will save you a lot of emotional turmoil. While some Flirts appear on the scene without warning, most do not. For example, you know who the Flirts are in your circle of friends. You've heard stories or noticed behaviors that tip you off. If your internal radar is correct, the best thing you can do is stay clear of Flirts. Don't allow yourself, or your spouse if that is the situation, to be caught alone with Flirts. Use any excuse— going to the rest room, for example — to avoid giving Flirts the opportunity to make a pass.

> **Facts do not cease to exist because they are ignored.**
> Aldous Huxley

Be Openly Affectionate with Your Spouse

If you are married (or in a serious dating relationship) and en-countering Flirts, you have at your disposal one of the most effective techniques for defusing coquettish behavior. Whether at work, at church, or anywhere else, this technique is one of your best bets for dousing Flirts' fire. Simply make a point of showing affection for your spouse or dating partner. If you are together, hold hands. If you are alone, keep talking about the one you love. Take preventative measures in your office by displaying plenty of pictures of your spouse or dating partner. And above all, never tease or criticize your spouse or dating partner in front of Flirts, who may read it as a sign that you're not happy with your spouse and who may, as the song says, start "looking for love."

Refuse to Be a Victim

An administrative assistant employed at W. R. Grace & Com-pany recalled the morning that her boss popped into her office unexpectedly. She offered to bring him some coffee. "When I bent down to put the cup on the credenza for him, he reached over and brushed his hand on my leg." This was no accident, she says. "When I looked at him, he had a Cheshire-cat grin on his face." In shock, she stalked out of the room and did nothing. Not surprisingly, her boss continued to do these kinds of things until, out of a sense of total helplessness, she quit. If Flirts are not confronted when they first exhibit inappropriate behavior, they will repeat the behavior. The point is that if you are not going to be a victim, you need to confront flirtatious behavior when it first occurs. To say nothing tells Flirts that you are fair game. Many women experience repeated scenes of uncomfortable behavior with Flirts because they haven't thought through their

> **Sensual pleasures are like soap bubbles, sparkling, effervescent. The pleasures of intellect are calm, beautiful, sublime, ever enduring and climbing upward to the borders of the unseen world.**
> **John H. Aughey**

feelings and because they simply haven't said stop. A *Working Woman* magazine survey shows that just 26 percent of women who say they've been the victim of an aggressive Flirt report the incident. The rest remain victims.

Have a Ready Comeback

If you encounter Flirts at work, use this line: "Hold on for a minute. Let's talk about what just happened, as two professionals." A statement like this doesn't require you to get huffy or preachy. But it immediately cools off the flirtatious ardor and puts you in charge. It brings whatever just happened to a rational and professional level. On top of that, the person will be surprised at how composed and together you are. This statement will startle Flirts into realizing you have no intentions of anything but a completely professional work situation. Simply saying "Hold on for a minute. Let's talk about this as two professional colleagues" allows you to reestablish the camaraderie that you will need in order to get this person to treat you as an equal.

Find a Good Comrade

In the comedy film *Frankie and Johnny,* a waitress named Frankie is asked by another waitress to help her handle a male customer who thinks he has the right to flirt with any woman who serves him food. Quickly, Frankie tells the other waitress, "You pour. I'll bump." Faking a collision, they drench the man's lap with ice water. While I don't necessarily recommend such drastic measures, I do recommend that you tell someone what behavior makes you uncomfortable. You need to have someone who is on your side. You deserve to have someone who knows what happened and who takes it seriously. You also deserve to have someone who supports you emotionally, someone who knows you don't deserve to be treated with disrespect.

Know What Sexual Harassment Is

Before the mid-1970s, sexual harassment probably was common, but people rarely used the term. People didn't know what to call overly flirtatious behavior and sexual aggression that belittled people. Once sexual harassment had a name, however, organizations attempted to define more specifically what it involved. One of the most common definitions appeared in the *Journal of Social Problems.* Sexual harassment is "behavior that includes verbal sexual suggestions or jokes; constant leering or ogling; 'accidental' brushing against a person's body; a 'friendly' pat or squeeze; putting an arm around the other person; catching the person alone for a quick kiss; the explicit proposition backed by threat of job loss; and forced sexual relations." This kind of behavior is a blight on society and wrong in any situation. Even if Flirts' comments and actions are disguised as flattery, they may fall into the category of sexual harassment. When this is the case, Flirts have not only violated your personal boundaries but also broken the law. It is at this point that you have every right to file a complaint with the State Department of Fair Employment or with the Federal Equal Employment Opportunity Commission, who will investigate your claim.

Fear is the sand in the machinery of life.
E. Stanley Jones

CROSS-REFERENCE

For more information related to Flirts, see these other high-maintenance relationships: the Chameleon, the Green-Eyed Monster, and the Steamroller.

16

THE CHAMELEON
Eager to Please and
Avoids Conflict

MONICA and Ellen were the best of friends, for about six weeks. They met at an orientation meeting for new employees at a downtown bank. All morning they listened to talks and watched videos about bank protocol and proper procedures.

At lunchtime, the two women ended up together at a deli. Monica was ordering a sardine sandwich when Ellen piped up, "I love sardines too."

"You're kidding me," said Monica. "I thought I was the only sardine lover on earth!"

They ended up sharing a sandwich and seemed to hit it off right from the beginning.

In the weeks that followed, Monica was struck by their similar tastes. She and Ellen shared a lot of the same interests and had a great time together—until Monica began to catch on. You see, whatever Monica liked, Ellen liked. Whatever Monica wanted to do, Ellen wanted to do. But it was more than that. Ellen was beginning to anticipate Monica's every need. Ellen bought her a toaster, for example, because Monica had mentioned in passing that hers was broken. Ellen gave her a subscription to a gardening magazine because Monica was thinking about growing some vegetables. It seemed Monica couldn't make a move or whisper a need without having Ellen try to respond. It began to feel eerie.

When two men in business always agree, one of them is unnecessary.
William Wrigley Jr.

That's when it happened. Monica confronted Ellen about the issue, and Ellen sobbed, "I thought we were friends. Why are you talking this way? Don't you like me?"

Monica felt terrible. "Of course I like you," she said, trying to console Ellen. "But you were driving me nuts."

Have you ever felt like Monica? If so, you know the challenge of relating to Chameleons, the people who lose their identity in trying to become whatever they think you want them to be. Like Monica, you were probably struck by how much you had in common with Chameleons, by how compatible you seemed to be. Compatibility, of course, is a fundamental building block to any successful relationship. Compatibility brings comfort, safety, and understanding.

But is it possible to have too much compatibility? Yes. Every growing relationship needs a little incompatibility, a little conflict to give it some life. That's why Chameleons can be so frustrating. After a while, their kindness feels stifling, suspiciously needy, and hollow.

Scottish historian Thomas Carlyle once said, "I don't like to talk much with people who always agree with me. It is amusing to coquette with an echo for a little while, but one soon tires of it." If you are like most people relating to Chameleons, you probably agree. This high-maintenance relationship can pump you with exhilaration and energy at first, but it soon becomes depleting. If you do not manage the relationship, it will bring you under.

THE ANATOMY OF A CHAMELEON

Of all the high-maintenance relationships discussed in this book, the Chameleon is one of the most deceptive. Why? Because it appears to be a low-maintenance relationship at first. Chameleons don't argue; they go with the flow. They are easy to get along with. But underlying their agreeable exterior is a complex web of distorted perceptions and insatiable longings. Chameleons, it turns out, require a great deal of attention. Chameleons are superagreeable, unreliable, overly dependent, compliant, insecure, prone to guilt, narrowly focused, and superficial.

There is no conversation more boring than the one where everybody agrees.
Michel de Montaigne

Superagreeable

"Sure, I can do that." "No problem, I'll be ready." "You bet I like it." These short one-liners fall out of the mouth of Chameleons one after the other. To avoid disappointing just about anyone, from an anonymous waitress to a close relative, Chameleons will agree with whatever seems appropriate. If you don't want pizza, neither do they. If you are too warm, they are too.

Unreliable

Eager to please, Chameleons often let other people down. They will make unrealistic commitments: "I'll have that report to you by tomorrow morning" or "I'll be home in less than an hour." They say it with sincerity and goodwill, but often they simply do not follow through. Eventually you learn they are unreliable. Their words do not match their deeds.

Overly Dependent

Because they toil tirelessly to please others, Chameleons can barely make a decision on their own. They depend, instead, on the social climate. If you won't make their decisions for them, they will study your face and try to determine what they think you want them to do. When Chameleons try to stand on their own two feet, they wobble.

Compliant

"Don't rock the boat." That's the motto by which Chameleons live. They avoid saying what they really think to escape potential conflict. It is as if a censor were working overtime in their head, editing and readapting the material they are willing to share with others. Why? Because Chameleons would rather die than have an argument.

Insecure

Chameleons take everything personally. If you respond to call waiting while you are talking with them on the phone, they feel slighted and conclude they must have said something to make you

Conform and be dull.
J. Frank Doble

unhappy with them. If you show up late for a lunch appointment, they are sure they have offended you. If you don't like their kids, they feel personal blame. If something goes wrong, they immediately assume something is wrong with them. Chameleons have a terminal case of insecurity.

Prone to Guilt

Chameleons carry a backpack filled with self-condemnation. "Why can't I be a better friend?" "If only I were not so bad at preparing meals." "I shouldn't let my disappointment show." Driven by a nagging conscience, Chameleons feel they never measure up.

Narrowly Focused

"It was good, but I undercooked the carrots," says the Chameleon after preparing a wonderful meal. It's insignificant, and nobody cares, but Chameleons draw attention to their foibles. They have a way of zeroing in on a single negative comment, for example, and blowing it out of proportion. One word of criticism can erase all the praise they received over the last month.

Superficial

Chameleons are consumed by the question. "What will people think?" It is a question they ask again and again, day after day. It serves as their antenna for detecting disapproval. "What will people think if I wear this or do that? Will they like me?" The result of this obsession is a superficiality that is concerned more with how they *look* than with who they *are*.

DO YOU KNOW A CHAMELEON?

The following self-test can help you assess whether you are in a high-maintenance relationship with a Chameleon. Identify the person or people who have come to your mind as you have read the preceding paragraphs. Circle the *Y* if the statement is true of the person or people about whom you are thinking. Circle the *N* if the statement does not apply to this person or people.

Y N   This person goes along with nearly everything I say.

Y N   Sometimes I feel as if our identities have melded.

Y N   This person's world revolves around pleasing others.

Y N   This person rarely says no.

Y N   After agreeing to do something, this person often doesn't follow through.

Y N   This person can't seem to make a decision on his or her own.

Y N   This person avoids conflict at all costs.

Y N   I sometimes feel this person is kind of hollow, focused exclusively on the exterior world.

Y N   This person takes things personally and gets his or her feelings hurt easily.

Y N   If something goes wrong, this person takes the blame.

Y N   This person seems to think I don't accept him or her when I really do.

Y N   This person can do something wonderful and then pinpoint a tiny, insignificant flaw and focus on it.

Y N   I get the feeling this person will change just about anything to make me happy.

Y N   This person agrees with almost everything I say.

Y N   This person craves approval from others.

Scoring: Total the number of *Y*s you circled. If you circled ten or more *Y*s, you are certainly in a high-maintenance relationship with a Chameleon.

UNDERSTANDING CHAMELEONS

Pulitzer prize-winning journalist Henry Bayard Swope once noted: "I cannot give you the formula for success, but I can give you the formula for failure: Try to please everybody." Chameleons do just that.

The need to please is at the core of Chameleons' identity. They dress to please, talk to please, and behave to please. They smile no matter what. They are terrified by the slightest possibility of snubbing someone or hurting someone's feelings. Approachable and ever agreeable, Chameleons are highly skilled at winning approval. Just as the desert craves the rain, Chameleons crave approval.

Crave may seem like a strong term, but only a powerful word such as *crave* adequately describes the powerful hold the need for approval has on Chameleons. They live in terrible fear of rejection.

For Chameleons, it all comes down to being accommodating. Chameleons readily adjust their own self-interest in order to take into account the interests of others. Out of habit, it seems, they offer the better seat in a movie theater to their companion, hold the door open for total strangers, share their last bit of candy with a friend. Common courtesy, we call it, but it's not so common anymore. Accommodation is an increasingly rare and wonderful civility these days, and Chameleons, at least to the untrained eye, offer a refreshing example of how it can be done. The problem with this accommodation, however, is that Chameleons have taken a good thing too far. Because they are addicted to approval, they overdose on accommodation. As a result, Chameleons exhibit a kind of deluded or false accommodation, in which their self-interest is never really set aside. *In actuality, they are not yielding to another so much out of goodwill as out of a fear of not being accepted.*

> I have never in my life learned anything from any man who agreed with me.
> Dudley Field Malone

Chameleons spend most of their waking hours worrying about whether people like them, agree with them, understand them, care about them, respect them, and admire them. They are possessed and obsessed with the idea that they must please everybody.

As a result, Chameleons march to the beat of everyone else's drum. They have a compliant personality and try desperately to make others happy. As children, their primary goal was not to be a cheerleader or be president of the class. Instead, they tried to make their parents happy.

To understand the inner workings of the Chameleon, we must realize that appearance is everything. Little else matters. Chameleons are wonderful actors and will change their role in an instant if they believe that is what you want. If they are feeling lighthearted and you are in the mood for a serious conversation, they will become serious (and vice versa). Whatever you want, they'll do their best to supply. They will even attempt to read your mind to detect your desires. This kind of conformity results in a hollow feeling of superficial relationships, built more on doing than being.

> **It is better to be hated for what you are than loved for what you are not.**
> André Gide

Chameleons' sense of inferiority is deeply ingrained because their self-worth is based on performance. They equate what you think of them —or, more accurately, what *they* think you think of them—with who they are.

COPING WITH CHAMELEONS

Being in a relationship with a Chameleon is like holding the acceleration pedal all the way down but keeping the car in neutral and a foot on the brake. It consumes your energy and takes you nowhere fast. If you are about to give up on a consuming Chameleon, however, don't. There are a number of proven strategies for improving this kind of relationship and getting it moving in the right direction.

Face the Chameleon Within

Maybe you are the assertive type. Maybe you don't struggle with expressing your true thoughts and feelings. But be honest. Haven't you had moments when you have buried your own wishes, smiled, and done what the other person wanted? Haven't you had situations in which you wanted someone to respect you so badly that you became superagreeable and compliant? Granted, this may not be your primary mode, but if you can remember what it feels like to be apprehensive about approval, you will have at least a bit of empathy for Chameleons. If nothing else, think about your most terrifying job interview, the time you really wanted the position and weren't very sure of your chances. That is just how Chameleons feel in nearly every interaction, day in and day out.

Take a Personal Interest

Chameleons become more candid when they feel understood. What do you really know about the Chameleons in your life? Are you sincerely interested in who they are and what they do? I once worked in a clinic that had a Chameleon for an office assistant. She was very pleasant and perfect with the patients. But she didn't always follow through on assignments. However, I noticed that she was following through for the director. It took me a while, but by following the clinic director's lead, I began to catch on to what made Cindy work. He wouldn't simply make requests of Cindy and then go about his business. He would ask her questions about her workload and upcoming projects. Then he would see if she could meet a deadline for something he needed. On top of that, he asked her about her weekend and showed a genuine interest in her well-being. Cindy welcomed his personal interest in her and began to follow through on the work he had asked her to do. If the Chameleons you encounter are at your workplace, ask them about their family. Find out what they are doing for their upcoming vacation. Make sure your interest is genuine. Chameleons are very good at detecting insincerity.

> **Now Peter was sitting out in the courtyard, and a servant girl came to him. "You also were with Jesus of Galilee," she said. But he denied it before them all. "I don't know what you're talking about," he said.**
> Matthew 26:69-70

Boost Their Self-Confidence with a Little Reassurance

Chameleons suffer from what experts call "communication apprehension." Afraid that they may say or do something socially unacceptable, Chameleons defer to others. For example, they will always let you choose the restaurant to avoid losing your favor ("What if they don't like the restaurant I choose?"). This deference is fueled by a low sense of self-worth. You can boost their self-confidence by affirming their decisions, no matter how small or seemingly insignificant those decisions are. Remember, Chameleons need to know that you accept them. The more they sense this, the more likely they are to take bigger risks and open up. If you want them to be more honest with you, reassure them on the small steps they take in that direction. When they risk being forthright, tell them you appreciate it. While Chameleons suffer from apprehension, they thrive on reassurance.

Steer Clear of Guilt Motivation

In his sermon "The Weight of Glory," C. S. Lewis warns of the dangers of being immoderately unselfish: "Unselfishness carries with it the suggestion not primarily of securing good things for others, but of going without them ourselves, as if our abstinence and not their happiness was the important point." Chameleons need to learn that being a good friend or a caring coworker is not about doing without. Self-denial may serve as a means to meeting another person's needs from time to time, but it should never serve as an end in itself. We can give our body to be burned, as Scripture says, and still not be loving (see 1 Cor. 13:3). Keep the Chameleon from falling into this trap by steering clear of guilt motivation. Remember that Chameleons are already driven by a nagging conscience.

> Adaptability is not imitation. It means power of resistance and assimilation.
> Mahatma Gandhi

Clarify Their Commitments

You can save yourself and Chameleons a great deal of anguish by questioning them about the commitments they want to make. For example, when they say they will be home in fifteen minutes and you suspect that's impossible with traffic, clarify: "Don't you think it will be more like thirty minutes at this time of day?" This gives Chameleons opportunity to face the facts instead of focusing entirely on your feelings. It gives Chameleons the chance to say something like, "You are probably right. It will be closer to thirty minutes." A simple clarification opens a small window for Chameleons to be more truthful. It may seem silly to you to have to clarify such small commitments, but remember that Chameleons are peacekeepers. Harmony is so important to them that they will deny or ignore that anything is ever wrong. They are more concerned about peace than about truth. So do yourself a favor and help to clarify Chameleons' commitments.

Ask for Honesty

"Say what you have to say, not what you ought," said Henry David Thoreau. That's hard advice for Chameleons to swallow. It's not that they want to be dishonest; they just don't want to offend anyone. For this reason Chameleons need a little nudge. Many times a straightforward request for an honest opinion is all that is required: "I really want to know what's on your mind. I value your honest feedback." An invitation to be honest, to speak their mind, is one thing Chameleons need to open up. So make it clear that their opinions or even their criticisms won't earn them your displeasure. For example, instead of saying, "What didn't you like about our proposal this morning?" say, "I'm really glad you like the proposal, but there have got to be some weak spots. Which parts do you think could be improved?" Even then you may have to keep prodding them. But the more often you invite them to be honest, the more candid they will be.

Be Ready for Burnout

Mahatma Gandhi said, "A 'No' uttered from deepest conviction is better and greater than a 'Yes' merely uttered to please, or what is worse, to avoid trouble." Chameleons, unfortunately, are more likely to dole out yesses to avoid risking rejection. They rarely say, "My

> It gives me great pleasure indeed to see the stubbornness of an incorrigible nonconformist warmly acclaimed.
> Albert Einstein

feelings got hurt when you . . ." or "I think we need to resolve this problem you and I are having." Chameleons will not confront conflict head-on. However, sooner or later Chameleons will be cornered and forced into conflict. At this point they usually give in ("I'm to blame; it's my fault"), but sometimes they will blow up. It's like the story of the little Texan boy who found a chameleon under a cactus and took it home for a pet. His greatest joy was to watch it change colors as he put it on pieces of red, green, or blue paper. Then one day he got a mean thought. He put the chameleon on a piece of Scotch plaid, and it blew up trying to be all colors at once. Overworked and exhausted Chameleons in your life just might do the same. So be ready.

CROSS-REFERENCE

For more information related to Chameleons, see these other high-maintenance relationships: the Gossip, the Martyr, and the Backstabber.

17

MAKING THE MOST OF EVERY RELATIONSHIP

DEALING effectively with high-maintenance relationships involves more than knowing when to set boundaries, more than when to confront, more than empathy, more than good communication skills. In other words, handling impossible people involves more than just *doing* certain things. It involves *being* a different person.

Author James A. Michener has made his mark in the literary world by producing massive historical novels such as *Hawaii, The Covenant, Texas,* and *Poland,* to name only a few. Michener's style has drawn its strength and beauty from characters fleshed out with extensive genealogy and deep cultural roots. Yet, ironically, Michener is a man without a birth certificate. Abandoned as an infant, raised as a foster son in the Michener family headed by a widowed woman, James never knew his biological parents. While he claims to have come to peace with this lack of knowledge, it is easy to see why he finds pleasure inventing extensive lineages for all his characters with each new novel.

Despite his generous spirit and kind nature, Michener's accomplishments raised the ire of one of his adoptive family members. In a rage of jealousy, mean-spiritedness, and sheer nastiness, some anonymous high-maintenance relative—self-signed "a real Michener"—felt compelled to write hate-filled, hurtful notes to James whenever his name gained fame or newspaper space. Even after Michener won a Pulitzer prize, this poison-pen writer charged Michener with besmirching the good Michener name—which he said, "You have no right to use"—and denounced him as a fraud. But the barb this anonymous person thrust the most deeply under Michener's skin was "Who do you think you are, trying to be better than you are?"

> We hardly find any persons of good sense save those who agree with us.
>
> François de La Rochefoucauld

The final letter James Michener received from his unknown relative came in 1976, after President Ford had presented James with the Presidential Medal of Freedom. The acidic note read, "Still using a name that isn't yours. Still a fraud. Still trying to be better than you are."

Michener testifies that the words of that note were "burned into my soul." But Michener turned the negative power of that accusation into a life challenge. Michener admits to missing the nasty letters when his relative presumably died: "He was right in all his accusations," Michener confessed. "I have spent my life trying to be better than I was, and I am a brother to all who share the same aspiration."[1]

If we are to make the most of even our troublesome, irritating, and difficult relationships, it will be because we are trying to be better than we are—it will be because we are aspiring to be the people God calls us to be. Jesus asks a pointed question about this issue in his Sermon on the Mount: "If you love those who love you, what reward will you get? . . . And if you greet only your brothers, what are you doing more than others? Do not even pagans do that? Be perfect, therefore, as your heavenly Father is perfect" (Matt. 5:46-48).

To be better than we are means taking the high road, choosing to love even impossible people. To be better than we are means choosing to become more Christlike in our patience, our compassion, our honesty, our willingness to extend grace, our ability to forgive.

In this final chapter, I leave you with a challenge—not to *do*, but to *be*. I challenge you to *be* better than you are, to *be* more Christlike by allowing him to cultivate in you four virtues: humility, determination, acceptance, and hope.

HUMILITY

Between two farms near Valleyview, Alberta, you can find two parallel fences, only two feet apart, running for a half mile. Why are there two fences when one would do? Because two farmers, Paul and Oscar, had a disagreement that erupted into a feud. Paul wanted to build a fence between their land and split the cost, but Oscar was unwilling to contribute. Since Paul wanted to keep cattle on his land, he went ahead and built the fence anyway.

After the fence was completed, Oscar said to Paul, "I see we have a fence."

"What do you mean 'we'?" Paul asked. "I got the property line surveyed and built the fence two feet into my land. That means some of my land is outside the fence. And if any of your cows set foot on my land, I'll shoot 'em."

> Give, and it will be given to you. A good measure, pressed down, shaken together and running over, will be poured into your lap. For with the measure you use, it will be measured to you. Luke 6:38

Oscar knew Paul wasn't joking, so when Oscar eventually decided to use the land adjoining Paul's for pasture, he was forced to build another fence, two feet away.

Oscar and Paul have both died, but their double fence stands as a monument to the high price we pay for pride. When it comes to handling high-maintenance relationships, it is tempting to follow their example and pride ourselves on how right we are or how clever we are. But of course, this is a lie. Pride, by definition, allows no room for humility. And there is no hope of change in ourselves or our relationships without humility. Ultimately, Scripture tells us, there is no hope of salvation without humility (see Matt. 18:3-4).

I don't know about you, but it often helps me to remember that just like the high-maintenance person who complicates my existence, I also am a difficult person. I too can be a Control Freak. I too can be a Wet Blanket. I too can be a Cold Shoulder. It's not easy to admit this, but I know that my confession is the first step on the road to humility. When I realize that I too am a high-maintenance person— to other people and especially to God— and when I realize

We cannot think, feel, will, or act without the perception of a goal. Alfred Adler

that they extend grace to me by loving me and staying in a relationship with me in spite of who I am, then I can extend that same grace to the impossible people in my life.

Humility greases the way for other virtues to follow. As William Gurnall put it, "Humility is the necessary veil to all other graces." Indeed, "God gives grace to the humble" (see James 4:6; 1 Pet. 5:5; Matt. 23:12).

DETERMINATION

In June of 1955, Winston Churchill, who was then near the end of his life, was asked to give a commencement address at a British university. He was physically weak and had to be helped to the podium. He stood with his head down, with his hands gripping the podium for what seemed an interminable amount of time.

Then he finally raised his great leonine head. The voice that years before had called Britain back from the brink of destruction sounded publicly for the last time in history: "Never give up. Never give up. Never give up."

With that, Churchill turned and went back to his seat. At first the audience sat in stunned silence. But then, as if one person, the whole audience rose to applaud the man and his words. Throughout Churchill's political career, he had known setbacks. Three times he was sent off to oblivion, and yet somehow he had the determination to go on, to trust that good would come out of difficult circumstances.

Churchill's determination and perseverance can serve as a model to all of us who want to make the most of every relationship. Why? Because when we are faced with a difficult person, most of us are tempted to give up and run for cover. But that's fatal. To have a fighting chance, every relationship needs determination—especially in times of frustration and conflict.

So in handling impossible people, we must not run from conflict. The Bible cites many examples of those who gave up and ran when they faced conflict. When Christ agonized in the Garden of Gethsemane, his disciples came with him to watch and pray. But they couldn't stay awake with their Lord. During the night Judas arrived with a "large crowd armed with swords and clubs" (Matt. 26:47). A confrontation erupted, and by the end of it, "all the disciples deserted him and fled" in fear (Matt. 26:56).

> When you are outraged by somebody's impudence, ask yourself at once, "Can the world exist without impudent people?" It cannot; so do not ask for impossibilities.
>
> Marcus Aurelius

Adam and Eve, Moses, David, Elijah, and Peter also tried to avoid conflict (see Gen. 3:8; Exod. 2:15; 1 Sam. 21:10; 1 Kings 19:3; Mark 14:68). As I said, the Bible is filled with very human examples that illustrate our lack of determination when it comes to difficult relationships. But if we are to be better than we are, we must resist this temptation. The truth is that many high-maintenance relationships improve, in great part, simply because one person was *determined* to make it better.

ACCEPTANCE

In my own attempt to be better than I am with difficult people, I find acceptance to be my biggest hurdle. I confess that it's much easier for me to diagnose, label, and pigeonhole impossible people than it is to look beyond their frailties and accept them for who they are. I want them to change, to alter their personality for me, and it's hard to surrender this desire.

Recently I read *The Whisper Test* by Mary Ann Bird. This story has become an inspiration to me in accepting others.

I grew up knowing I was different, and I hated it. I was born with a cleft palate, and when I started school, my classmates made it clear to me how I looked to others: a little girl with a misshapen lip, crooked nose, lopsided teeth, and garbled speech.

When schoolmates asked, "What happened to your lip?" I'd tell them I'd fallen and cut it on a piece of glass. Somehow it seemed more acceptable to have suffered an accident than to have been born different. I was convinced that no one outside my family could love me.

There was, however, a teacher in the second grade whom we all adored—Mrs. Leonard by name. She was short, round, happy—a sparkling lady.

Annually we had a hearing test. . . . Mrs. Leonard gave the test to everyone in the class, and finally it was my turn. I knew from past years that as we stood against the door and covered one ear, the teacher sitting at her desk would whisper something, and we would have to repeat it back—things like "The sky is blue" or "Do you have new shoes?" I waited there for those words that God must have put into her mouth, those seven words that changed my life. Mrs. Leonard said, in her whisper, "I wish you were my little girl."

The acceptance Mrs. Leonard showed Mary Ann Bird is the same acceptance I want to show the people I encounter— including impossible people. I don't always succeed, but even when I am trying, I gain a sense of peace. In other words, my attempts at accepting difficult people diminish my disappointment in the relationship and allow me to arm myself in advance against repeated bruises. I have a friend, for example, who is always late, and it used to make me angry with him. But rather than getting bent out of shape and trying to change him, I practice acceptance by bringing along a book when I am to meet him. If I give him a manuscript to read and he promises to look at it over the weekend, I prepare for a month-long wait. Accepting him and his irritating behavior lessens my frustration and takes the pressure off the relationship.

Each of you should look not only to your own interests, but also to the interests of others.
Philippians 2:4

The term *acceptance* comes from the Latin *ad capere,* meaning "to take to oneself." In other words, inherent in the process of offering acceptance to difficult people is the act of *receiving* acceptance ourselves. That's where God's grace once again becomes evident. In spite of all our foibles, God offers us acceptance that we could never earn. Once we receive his acceptance, we become better able to offer this same acceptance to others.

Acceptance and grace can help every high-maintenance relationship be better than it is. So pray a slight modification of Niebuhr's well-known serenity prayer: "God give me grace to accept with serenity the impossible people whom I cannot change."

HOPE

Once you have humbly admitted your own high-maintenance personality, once you have determined to make your relationships work, and once you have accepted other difficult people, you are ready for hope. This virtue, however, is not tagged on the end of this list because it sounds nice. Hope is a powerful force in the healing and nurturing of every difficult relationship. When things get dark, hope sheds light.

> **Goodness consists not in the outward things we do but in the inward things we are.**
> Edwin Hubbel Chapin

On a recent trip to London I visited the British Museum, where I discovered an unusual painting called *Hope.* On the background of this canvas were the familiar outlines of the continents and oceans of planet Earth. In the foreground was a beautiful woman seated at a harp. Nearly all of the harp's strings dangled helplessly from the top of the harp or lay uselessly on the lap of the woman's dress. Only one string remained taut.

My traveling companion commented on how little of the harp was still intact and said, "I wonder why they call the painting *Hope?*" The answer was clear to me. Hope is the song of a broken instrument. It is the plucking of that one string and knowing that you can still have music.

I think Augustine would have understood this painting's title too. He defined hope as having "two beautiful daughters. Their names are anger and courage; anger at the way things are, and courage to see that they do not remain the way they are." Surely Augustine must have encountered a few high-maintenance relationships.

Hope is what empowers us to draw on our reservoir of determination and make a commitment to accept an impossible person. Hope transforms. The New Testament writers consistently link hope to the transforming resurrection of Jesus. Peter opens his first letter this way: "Praise be to the God and Father of our Lord Jesus Christ! In his great mercy he has given us new birth into a living hope through the resurrection of Jesus Christ from the dead" (1 Pet. 1:3).

Without hope, high-maintenance relationships become a living hell. Dante tells us that the sign that hangs over the entrance of hell reads, "Abandon hope, ye who enter here."

Don't jettison your hope of making yourself and your relationships better than they are. Don't convince yourself that a difficult person is forever impossible. Keep the spirit of hope alive. Ed Delavega did. He was a dentist in South Central Los Angeles when the 1991 riots occurred. Most of his office was burned, but on what remained, he painted: "You burned my place, but *not* my spirits."

I remind you of my challenge: Don't let a high-maintenance relationship burn your opportunity to be better than you are. Don't let a difficult relationship dampen the process of living a holy life. Make the most of every relationship through humility, determination, acceptance, and hope.

A FINAL THOUGHT

An ancient tale describes a young girl walking through a meadow when she sees a butterfly impaled on a thorn. Artfully, she releases the butterfly, which starts to fly away. Then it comes back, changed into a beautiful fairy. "For your kindness," the fairy tells the little girl, "I will grant your fondest wish."

The little girl thinks for a moment and replies, "I want to be happy." The fairy leans toward her, whispers in her ear, and then suddenly vanishes.

As the girl grew, no one in the land was more happy than she.

Whenever anyone asked her for the secret of her happiness, she would only smile and say, "I listened to a good fairy."

As she grew old, the neighbors were afraid the fabulous secret might die with her. "Tell us, please," they begged. "Tell us what the fairy said."

The lovely old lady simply smiled and said, "She told me that everyone, no matter how they appear, has need of me!"

This secret just may be the key to helping you make the best of your high-maintenance relationships. Whether you are coping with overagreeable friends, a controlling spouse, envious employees, critical colleagues, angry relatives, insensitive bosses, or any other impossible person— no matter how annoying—remember: they have need of you.

ENDNOTES

CHAPTER 1—ARE YOU IN A HIGH-MAINTENANCE RELATIONSHIP?
1. M. Sinetar, *Do What You Love and the Money Will Follow: Discovering Your Right Livelihood* (New York: Dell Publishing, 1987).
2. G. Myers, *The Pursuit of Happiness: Discovering the Pathway to Fulfillment, Well-being and Enduring Personal Joy* (New York: Avon Books, 1992).
3. All of the twenty-four high-maintenance relationships on the survey were ranked high by at least one person.

CHAPTER 2—THE CRITIC
1. William Glasser, *Control Theory: A New Explanation of How We Control Our Lives* (New York: Harper & Row, 1984), 159.
2. E. Stanley Jones, *The Way* (New York: Doubleday, 1978).
3. Deborah Tannen, *You Just Don't Understand: Women and Men in Conversation* (New York: Ballantine Books, 1990).

CHAPTER 3—THE MARTYR
1. Carla Perez, *Getting Off the Merry-Go-Round* (Greenwich, Conn.: Impact Publishers, 1994).
2. Lesley Hazleton, *The Right to Feel Bad* (New York: Ballantine, 1984).
3. M. Scott Peck, *The Road Less Traveled* (New York: Simon and Schuster, 1978).

CHAPTER 4—THE WET BLANKET
1. John P. Kildahl, *Beyond Negative Thinking* (New York: Avon Books, 1992).
2. Jennifer Crocker and Ian Schwarts, *Personality and Social Psychology Bulletin* 11, no. 4 (1986).
3. Brian Murphy and Howard Poilio, "I'll Laugh If You Will," *Psychology Today* (December 1973): 106–110.

CHAPTER 6—THE GOSSIP
1. M. E. Jaeger et al., "Gossip, Gossipers and Gossipees," *Good Gossip*, ed. R.S. Goodman and A. Ben-Zéeur (Lawrence, Kans.: University Press), 154–168.
2. Donna Eder, "The Structure of Gossip: Opportunities and Constraints on Collective Expressions Among Adolescents," *American Sociological Review* 56 (1991): 494–508.

3. Jack Levine, "Gossip: Media Small Talk," *Journal of Communication* 27 (1977): 169–173

CHAPTER 7—THE CONTROL FREAK
1. Judith Rodin, "Health and Aging," an address given to the Society of Behavioral Medicine, in Boston, 1988.
2. Meyer Friedman and Ray H. Rosenman, *Type A Behavior and Your Heart* (New York: Knopf, 1974).

CHAPTER 8—THE BACKSTABBER
1. Pat Springle, *Trusting: Learning Who and How to Trust Again* (Ann Arbor, Mich.: Servant, 1994).
2. David Augsburger, *Caring Enough to Confront* (Scottsdale, Ariz.: Herald Press, 1980).

CHAPTER 11—THE VOLCANO
1. David Stoop and Stephen Arterburn, *The Angry Man* (Waco, Tex.: Word, 1991).
2. L. R. Huesmann, "Stability of Aggression over Time and Generations," *Developmental Psychology* 20 (1984): 1120–34.

CHAPTER 12—THE SPONGE
1. Jonathan D. Brown and Tracie A. Mankowski, "Self-Esteem, Mood, and Self-Evaluation: Changes in Mood and the Way You See You," *Journal of Personality & Social Psychology* 64 (1993): 421.
2. Carmen Renee Berry, *When Helping You Is Hurting Me* (San Francisco: Harper Collins, 1989).
3. Erma Bombeck, *I Want to Grow Hair, I Want to Grow Up, I Want to Go to Boise* (New York: Harper & Row, 1989), 56–57.

CHAPTER 13—THE COMPETITOR
1. Janet Spence, "Achievement Motivation and Scientific Attainment," *Personality and Social Psychology Bulletin* 4 (1978): 222–226.
2. Alfie Kohn, *No Contest* (Boston: Houghton Mifflin, 1992).

CHAPTER 14—THE WORKHORSE
1. David Burns, *Feeling Good: The New Mood Therapy* (New York: Signet, 1980).
2. Gordon MacDonald, *Ordering Your Private World* (Nashville: Thomas Nelson, 1995).
3. Daniel Levinson, *Seasons of a Man's Life* (New York: Ballantine, 1986).

CHAPTER 15—THE FLIRT
1. Richard Lacayo, "Tales from the Elevator," *Time* (17 April 1995): 51.

CHAPTER 17—MAKING THE MOST OF EVERY RELATIONSHIP
1. James Michener, *The World Is My Home: A Memoir* (New York: Random House, 1991), 484–486.

ABOUT THE AUTHOR

Dr. Les Parrott III is a professor of psychology and codirector with his wife, Dr. Leslie Parrott, of the Center for Relationship Development at Seattle Pacific University. He is a fellow in medical psychology at the University of Washington School of Medicine, and he is an ordained minister in the Church of the Nazarene. Dr. Parrott earned his M.A. in theology and his Ph.D. in clinical psychology from Fuller Theological Seminary. He is the author of more than fifty articles in such magazines as *Christianity Today, Marriage Partnership, Aspire, Moody, Christian Counseling Today,* and *Focus on the Family.* Les and Leslie live in Seattle, Washington.